Medieval Grave Slabs of County Tipperary, 1200 – 1600 A.D.

Denise Maher

BAR British Series 262
1997

Published in 2019 by
BAR Publishing, Oxford

BAR British Series 262

Medieval Grave Slabs of County Tipperary, 1200 - 1600 A.D.

ISBN 9780860549239 paperback
ISBN 9781407318912 e-book

DOI https://doi.org/10.30861/9780860549239

A catalogue record for this book is available from the British Library

This book is available at www.barpublishing.com

BAR Publishing is the trading name of British Archaeological Reports (Oxford) Ltd. British Archaeological Reports was first incorporated in 1974 to publish the BAR Series, International and British. In 1992 Hadrian Books Ltd became part of the BAR group. This volume was originally published by John and Erica Hedges in conjunction with British Archaeological Reports (Oxford) Ltd / Hadrian Books Ltd, the Series principal publisher, in 1997. This present volume is published by BAR Publishing, 2019.

BAR titles are available from:

BAR Publishing
122 Banbury Rd, Oxford, OX2 7BP, UK
EMAIL info@barpublishing.com
PHONE +44 (0)1865 310431
FAX +44 (0)1865 316916
www.barpublishing.com

This book is dedicated to the memory of Ann Cashman-Maher

TABLE OF CONTENTS

Acknowledgements

The author wishes to express her sincere gratitude to the following people: Professor Peter Woodman, Department of Archaeology, University College Cork, and Mr Patrick Maher, her father, for their support and encouragement; Mr John Sheehan, Department of Archaeology, University College Cork, for his advice and endless patience, and Ms. Angela Desmond, Department of Archaeology, University College Cork, for preparing the layout of this publication. She also wishes to thank Ms. Rhoda Cronin, Lausanne, Switzerland, for preparing Figs. 4, 5, 6, 7, 8, 10, 11, 12, 14, 15, 16, 17, 18, 20 and 23; Mr Joe Kenny, Fethard, Co. Tipperary, for his photography (Figs. 1, 3, 21, 22 and 24-56); Ms. Nyree Finlay, Department of Archaeology, University College Cork, for preparing Fig. 2, and Ms. Geraldine Murphy, Cork, for assistance with preparing the distribution maps.

List of Figures

Fig. 1: Three medieval grave-slabs located in a tomb niche at Kilcooley Cistercian Abbey, Co. Tipperary (left to right, No's 1, 2 and 3).

CHAPTER ONE

INTRODUCTION

Despite their common occurrence in county Tipperary, medieval grave-slabs have received very little attention there. One hundred and seven such slabs have been recorded in the county during the course of the present study, and the fact that only thirty-six of these have been previously recorded indicates the low level of attention that this monument type has received to date. These are distributed over twenty-two sites, including cathedrals, monasteries and parish churches. The primary aim of this study is to record all surviving grave-slabs dating to between 1200 and 1600 A.D. from Tipperary. This work is presented in the Catalogue, the aim of which is not merely to record the form, decoration and inscriptions of the slabs but also to record their location and state of preservation. These results were achieved by extensive fieldwork and bibliographic research.

Why Tipperary? It is a critical area in which to study medieval cultural expression and change in Ireland primarily because of the fact that during much of this period its boundaries encompassed two discreet, but related, worlds - those of the Anglo-Norman newcomers and of the native Irish. The resultant interface, with its cultural, political and economic implications, makes Tipperary a county of contrasts. Topographically, it is also a diverse county, and its location within Ireland, "uneasily poised between the hinterlands of Cork, Limerick, Waterford and Dublin, but never dominated by them" (Whelan 1985, 215), makes it the geographical cockpit of the country (Fig. 2).

This study is divided into seven chapters. This introductory chapter aims to outline this approach and to consider work which has been previously done on the subject of medieval grave-slabs in general. The purpose of Chapter Two is to identify the cultural and historical background of this material by outlining and discussing the historical and archaeological background of medieval Tipperary. This involves a consideration of the origins of the county itself, the process of Anglo-Norman settlement in it following the invasion, the Gaelic resurgence of the fourteenth and later centuries and the role of the church. This background should serve to place the issues dealt with in other chapters in their proper perspective.

Chapter Three involves a discussion of the groups of grave-slabs within the county. By definition, a medieval grave-slab is a grave-cover or marker which features as its principal design a cross. The form of the cross can vary from a simple example with fleur-de-lis terminals to the more elaborate seven-armed fleur-de-lis type. There is quite a variety of cross-head types and these form the principle features which are used to classify the material into seven separate groupings. These groupings are then discussed with regard to their dating, distribution and cultural contexts.

Chapter Four deals specifically with the various motifs, emblems and symbols which occur on the grave-slabs, identifying the range and frequency of occurrence of these designs. Where possible they are compared with examples from elsewhere in Ireland and Britain. The material considered here includes heraldic devices, passion symbols, the standard Anglo-Norman designs of many of the slabs and the appearance of Celtic revival motifs on some of them.

Inscriptions are a very important aspect of medieval grave-slabs from the point of view of both dating and the historical information they provide. These inscriptions are discussed in Chapter Five. The various types of inscriptions and letter-forms are identified. Each individual inscription is listed, with a translation, in the relevant catalogue entries and this chapter examines their content with various questions in mind. These questions include the types of people commemorated by the slabs, their background and social significance. The question of whether a general development in the inscriptions can be identified is also addressed.

The purpose of Chapter Six is to propose a chronological sequence of development for the Tipperary grave-slabs. This is based on the overall form of the slabs, as well as on the nature and type of their inscriptions. The influence of each type on the others is considered, as is the extent of outside and native influences.

The concluding chapter investigates the social significance of the grave-slabs. It then places this in the context of the social, cultural, political and economic conditions of the period.

PREVIOUS WORK

One of the major problems which needs to be addressed in any study of Medieval Ireland is the lack of work which has been carried out in the era. There are historical reasons for this void. The growth of medieval archaeology as a discipline in Ireland has been somewhat retarded because of current political circumstances. During the first fifty years of Independence, Irish scholars tended to look to the pre-Norman period as the primary area for research, resulting in a certain level of stagnation of medieval Irish history, archaeology and related disciplines. It can be stated with some justification that more work was done on Irish medieval grave-slabs during the nineteenth than the twentieth century.

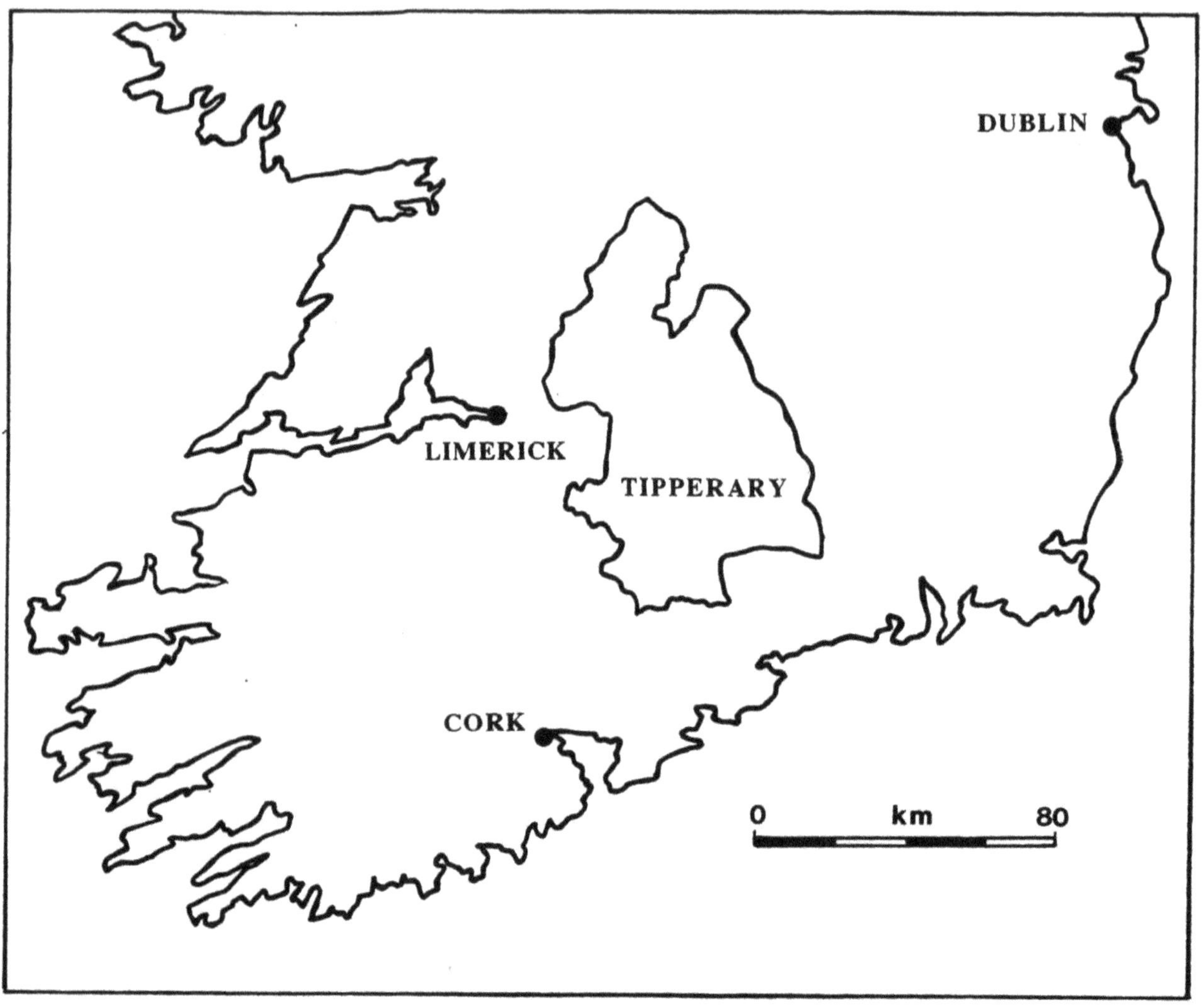

Fig. 2 Location map showing county Tipperary

In the past thirty years, however, a change in emphasis has occurred. A more pluralistic aspect to Irish society, combined with Ireland's increasing involvement in the European and World communities, have contributed towards an increasing interest in all aspects of medieval Ireland. Initially, however, this interest in the discipline of archaeology was directed towards standing monuments, such as castles, monasteries and towns. To date medieval archaeology has not significantly progressed beyond this stage, with little work being done on the lesser monuments. It is hoped that the present study will contribute in some way towards redressing this imbalance.

Recumbent grave-slabs are the most common medieval sepulchral monument to survive in Ireland, yet there has been no comprehensive work done on them. However, there have been a number of passing references and short articles published regarding certain slabs in specific sites. These have been published in the main archaeological journals, in the *Journal of the Association for the Preservation of the Memorials of the Dead, Ireland*, and in some of the regional journals. Many of these references, particularly the earlier ones, represent work done by local historians and antiquarians and are not of a consistently high standard.

Unfortunately, the study of sepulchral monuments often takes second place to that of the architecture of sites in which they are normally located. Consequently, they are usually only mentioned in passing. Very often they are studied only for the historical evidence contained in their inscriptions, and rarely is a more detailed study of their art or form engaged in. Very few attempts have been made to describe those medieval grave-slabs which have no inscriptions on them, with the exception of Bradley (1985). As Hunt noted (1974, 1), it was Mlle Duport who first voiced the necessity for the study of Irish medieval art (1934, 49-62). Thirty years later another plea was made by Helen M. Roe in her Royal Society of Antiquaries' Presidential Address (1966). Roe herself subsequently produced a number of publications which together form an invaluable contribution to medieval studies in general. Possibly the earliest discussion of a body of medieval sepulchral monuments was carried out in her 1968 article on cadaver effigial monuments. Here she not only draws attention to the carved tomb cover of Stamullen, Co. Meath, with its rare type of funerary effigy, but also to the role and concept of death in medieval Ireland (Roe 1968). She stresses that it is important to understand such a concept before attempting to understand the monuments.

In 1974 John Hunt published the first relevant major work on a national scale, entitled *Irish Medieval Figure Sculpture 1200-1600 A.D.* This two-volume work consists of descriptions and illustrations of almost three hundred monuments. The publication confines itself, however, to tombs dating to between 1200 and 1600 A.D. which feature carved figure sculpture and thus the vast majority of Ireland's medieval grave-slabs are not included. Hunt chronologically groups the monuments and, while he deals mainly with effigial tombs, his work is nevertheless useful for general parallels with certain types of grave-slabs, especially for 'head-slabs' and incised effigies.

The first study of a group of Irish medieval grave-slabs which went beyond the mere recording of their inscriptions was carried out by John Bradley in 1985. Dealing with the material from St. Canice's Cathedral, Kilkenny, it consists of eighty-nine catalogue entries. The detail in each entry is brief. Overall the study was not intended to be a comprehensive report, rather a general catalogue of the grave-slabs with some introductory points about their form, date and historical information. Even though this publication only concerns itself with the grave-slabs at one particular site, it does provide a useful foundation for further studies in Ireland.

In Britain, however, the amount that has been published on related material of the corresponding period is much more impressive. Major works include *Sepulchral Monuments in Great Britain*, an eighteenth-century publication by James Gough. As is the case with Hunt's *Irish Medieval Figure Sculpture*, however, this work deals largely with monumental effigies rather than grave-slabs. In 1849 the Rev. E.L. Cutts published *A Manual for the Study of Sepulchral Slabs and Crosses of the Middle Ages*, while another clergyman, C. Boutell, published *Christian Monuments in England and Wales*. These two works were to form an important basis for future studies. A number of other publications dealing with medieval cross-slabs appeared in Britain in the early twentieth century, including Styan's *History of Sepulchral Cross-Slabs* (1902). This book, which does not go into the subject in any great detail, comprises a catalogue of sixty-four grave-slabs which are mainly from the south of England. The excellent collection of drawings contained in it is useful for comparative purposes.

Probably the only major work published on medieval grave-slabs in Britain in recent years was written by Dr. L.A.S. Butler. His work on the subject in the 1950s culminated in his 'Minor Medieval Monumental Sculpture in the East Midlands', published in the *Archaeological Journal* (1964). One interesting and important result of this work is Butlers' recognition of local 'schools' of slab production. However, his proposed chronological scheme for these groups of slabs, based on stylistic evidence, is rather narrow.

The most recent work specifically on medieval grave-slabs to be carried out in Britain is Ryder's publication, *The Medieval Cross Slab Grave Cover in County Durham* (1985). This is a comprehensive and informative work which includes a catalogue of five hundred and fifty slabs, supplemented by numerous illustrations. Ryder gives a good account of cross design and proposes a scheme of chronological development for the material. It is important that such proposed developments in cross design be outlined in any study of medieval grave-slabs, so that an overall pattern in Ireland and Britain can be eventually established. Finally, Butler published a more specific article entitled 'Symbols on Medieval Memorials' in the *Archaeological Journal* (1987). This is an interesting and relevant work which discusses pagan versus Christian symbolism, symbolism of the clergy versus that of the laity, and contains a brief account of what the cross as a motif represents.

Any iconographical study of medieval grave-slabs which has the purpose of attaining a deeper understanding of medieval society and culture is an important contribution to medieval studies. Unfortunately, as can be seen from the above review, such work is scarce in England, and is virtually non-existent in Ireland.

* * * *

Medieval grave-slabs from county Tipperary have been published in both local historical works and journals. The latter are the more common sources of reference. None of the publications mentioned below can be classed as comprehensive studies, however, rather their main purpose was obviously to record the inscriptions on the slabs. The earliest publication of medieval grave-slabs from the county is contained in the *Journal of the Kilkenny Archaeological Society* (1855). In this article two grave-slabs, one from Cloneen and one from Drangan, both of seventeenth century date, were recorded by Brennan - a local classical teacher. In the same *Journal* for 1862-64, Brennan also published some seventeenth-century grave-slabs from Fethard Abbey.

Perhaps the most important journal for the purpose of this study is the *Journal of the Association for the Preservation of the Memorials of the Dead.* This *Journal* is of immense value in two ways: firstly, it assists in the compilation of general distributions and, secondly, the recorded inscriptions which it details are of invaluable assistance as many of these slabs are too worn to decipher today. The importance of its contribution to the recording of medieval sepulchral monuments cannot be emphasised enough.

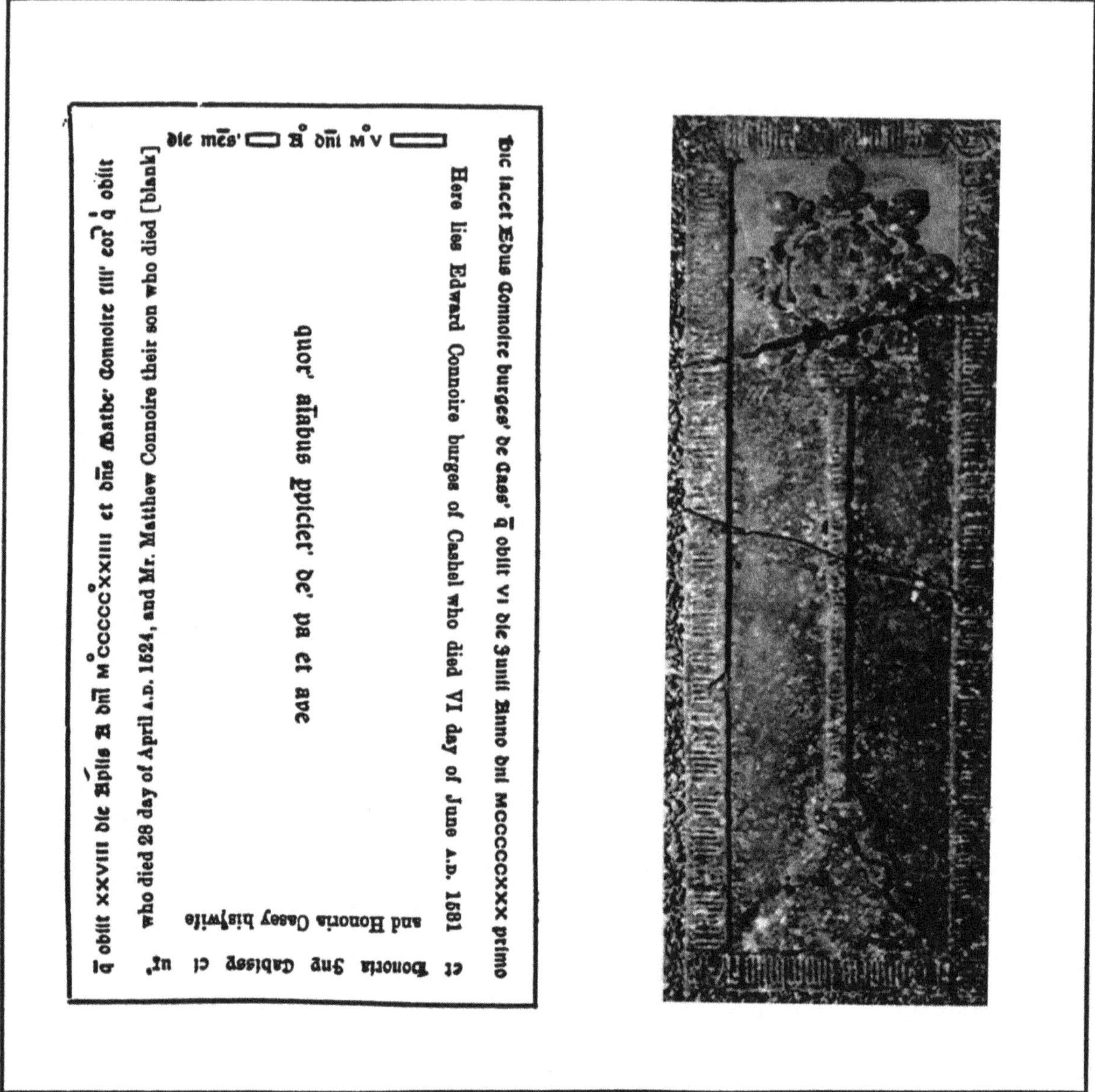

Fig. 3: St Patrick's Cathedral, Cashel 4: left, illustration of the slab after Fitzgerald 1903; right, photograph of the slab.

References to Tipperary grave-slabs start in the 1890 edition of the *Journal*, with an account of sixteenth-century tombstone inscriptions from the Franciscan Friary and Old St. Mary's, Clonmel. This information was contributed by two locals, Mr Clarke and Mrs Bagwell. In 1891 the Rev. R.H. Long gave an account of the graveyards in Fethard Parish but did not, however, include the medieval grave-slabs. Professor Stephens recorded an inscription from the sixteenth-century tombstone of Robertus Nale in the Fethard Abbey church, published in 1896. Probably the earliest instance of a recorded inscription occurs in the 1898 edition, in which inscriptions from sixteenth- and eighteenth-century tombstones from Knockgraffon graveyard were transcribed from an 1840 Ordnance Survey letter of John O'Donovan.

Lord Walter Fitzgerald, who was editor of the *Journal* for seventeen years, also made some valuable contributions on the subject of Tipperary slabs. In 1901 he published the Holy Cross burial monuments of the sixteenth and seventeenth centuries. In the following year he published the seventeenth-century monuments from both St. John's Cathedral, Cashel, and Loughmore graveyard. Finally, in this year also John Hewetson published the "O Donill" inscription at Clonmel. The following year, 1903, also saw a rich contribution from Tipperary, with Lord Walter Fitzgerald publishing all the medieval grave-slabs from St. Patrick's Cathedral, Cashel, the Rev. William Carrigan publishing the fifteenth- and sixteenth-century slabs from Kilcooley and John R. Garstin publishing the well-known sixteenth-century Hackett and Rochel tomb at the Holy Trinity church, Fethard. In 1907 the Rev. R.H. Long published the remainder of medieval grave-slabs from this Fethard site.

The number of contributions from elsewhere in Ireland over the following years was very small. In 1923 Lord Walter Fitzgerald died and this was a great blow to the society. The period between

1921-25 was also a troubled time for the *Journal*, with many of its records being destroyed as a result of the political disturbances. However, contributors were nonetheless encouraged to keep the *Journal* going. In 1926 it changed its title to the *Journal of the Irish Memorials Association*, and in 1930 the Hackett and Rochel tomb of Holy Trinity Church, Fethard, was published by E.A. Hackett. The *Journal* ceased publication in the late 1930s.

Even though the *Journal* is basically a catalogue of inscriptions, it does serve an important role in medieval grave-slab studies. Unfortunately, however, there are very few drawings contained in its issues and those that do occur were very often schematised. The illustration published by Fitzgerald of slab no. 4 at St. Patrick's Cathedral, Cashel, for instance, bears little resemblance to its subject (see Fig. 3). In some cases the published readings are inaccurate, with the 'correct' Latin forms given rather than the originals with their inaccuracies and misspellings. Accuracy of transcription often depended on the scholarship and dedication of the contributors in each area.

In 1928, O'Leary published the seventeenth-century Everard tombstone from the Holy Trinity church, Fethard. This publication also included a brief description of the slab. The Tipperary slabs were ignored over the following fifty years, until 1980 when the seventeenth-century tomb-slab at Lorrha was published by O'Farrell. Since then the slabs at Derrynaflan and Lisronagh have been published by Maher (1992, 1994).

The earliest local history book to incorporate a section on Tipperary grave-slabs is *Fethard: Its Abbey, etc.*, published by Knowles in 1903. This work is valuable in that many of the inscriptions which it records are illegible today. While it is also useful for the historical evidence it provides on some of the families mentioned in the inscriptions, it lacks any great detail about other aspects of the slabs themselves. Overall the work is rather romanticised, and the record of the inscriptions is only given in English. In addition, no illustrations accompany it.

A more recent booklet which includes a treatment of a group of Tipperary grave-slabs is that by W.J. Hayes (1970). In his work, entitled *Burials in Holycross Abbey,* the grave-slabs are catalogued in chronological order. Again the emphasis is on the historical evidence gleaned from the inscriptions, which are individually recorded.

Overall, the main purpose of medieval grave-slab studies conducted in Ireland up to the 1980s was to record the inscriptions for their historical evidence and, more importantly, for the preservation for posterity of the monuments. Bradley's work on the St. Canice's slabs in the 1980s was the only study which incorporated a discussion on the non-historical aspects. There have been a few articles written in the 1980s and 1990s, however, which, although not a study of medieval grave-slabs as such, are nonetheless very relevant to this subject. In 1985, for example, Gillespie's article entitled 'Funerals and Society in Early Seventeenth Century Ireland', discussed the heraldic, religious and social significance of late medieval funerals. Even though this is outside of the chronological context of this subject, it is still relevant as some of its arguments apply to the previous century. Gillespie also published another article, entitled 'The Image of Death, 1500-1700'. Here, he once again uses the funerary monuments to understand the "values and priorities of a society and not just its religious beliefs" (1992, 8).

All of the publications on the medieval grave-slabs of Tipperary - be they written by antiquarians at the turn of the century or by more recent local historians and archaeologists - form an important basis to any in-depth study on this subject.

CHAPTER TWO

MEDIEVAL TIPPERARY: THE ARCHAEOLOGICAL AND HISTORICAL BACKGROUND

The term "medieval" is of elastic application but for the purposes of this publication it is taken to refer to a period of some four hundred years commencing at the end of the twelfth century. The bulk of the archaeological evidence for this period takes the form of the many ruins and earthworks which occupy the landscape, for example those of parish churches, cathedrals, religious houses, tower houses, castles, moated sites, mottes and baileys and towns. County Tipperary has an unusually large number of such medieval monuments, comprising a rich source for the study of the social, cultural, economic and religious changes of the medieval period in the area.

The origins of this period began with the arrival of the Anglo-Normans to Ireland in 1169 and over the following decades. The conquest and consolidation took place between 1170 and 1330, a period which also saw a "wave of new religious foundations and reconstructions of many existing cathedrals" (Stalley 1971, 7). Along with various ecclesiastical reforms (which were initiated in the early twelfth century by Malachy) a whole new settlement pattern was introduced which was characterised by intensive agriculture. The newly-formed towns were of great importance as they provided the market-places for the produce from the estate manors, thus forming the basis of the Anglo-Norman economy.

It was really only in the early years of the thirteenth century that large-scale building in stone began to take place (Stalley 1971, 5), involving a striking expansion in both ecclesiastical and secular architecture. It is from this period onwards that effigies, carved tombs and grave-slabs become common features of ecclesiastical sites. Such sepulchral monuments commemorated both ecclesiastics and secular people of high social standing (as will be shown in later chapters). Therefore it should not be surprising to find that the distribution of such monuments and the occasional fusion of native and Anglo-Norman elements in them is very much linked to the rise, establishment and decline of the colony in Ireland.

The 'middle ages' was not all innovation and development. The invasion by Edward Bruce (1315-1318) and the Black Death (1348-49) recall Stalley's comment that "the sterility of Irish architecture in the mid-fourteenth century comes as no surprise" (1971, 148). New architectural projects diminished dramatically following the thirteenth century climax. Despite the fact that the Black Death, the plagues which followed it and local wars resulted in a dramatic rise in the number of deaths, a consequent increase in the production of sepulchral monuments was not the case, presumably due to the dramatic decline in the economic and psychological fortunes of the colony.

The fifteenth century saw a revival of native culture and language as well as an expansion in architecture and stone carving, especially in north Leinster and in Kilkenny, Waterford and Tipperary. Architectural expressions of this revival include masons' marks in the form of 'Celtic' knots and other interlaced motifs which are abundant in abbeys, for example those at Hore, Holycross, Fethard and Kilcooley (Stalley 1987, figs 6-8; Maher 1990, 35-41). Parallels for such motifs also occasionally occur on medieval grave-slabs, as on the example from Lisronagh (Maher 1992, 30-37).

After 1536, whilst the Reformation was taking place in England, Henry VIII brought about the decline of the great Anglo-Norman Geraldine family. He also took over Irish monastic lands in the ensuing years. Such measures undoubtedly brought about a general decline, not only in cultural matters, but also in ecclesiastical architecture and stonework. Throughout the period of the Tudor reigns the results of the Reformation included religious oppression and a dampening of native culture. By 1603 the dynamisms of both Gaelic and Anglo-Norman Ireland had effectively been brought to an end (Hunt 1974, 12).

THE ORIGINS OF TIPPERARY COUNTY

The medieval county of Tipperary formed part of the kingdom of Limerick, being settled by the Anglo-Normans in the period commencing in 1185. Most of the county was granted by King John to three individuals: Theobald Walter, ancestor to the Butlers, was given north and much of central Tipperary (comprising the modern baronies of Upper and Lower Ormond, Ikerrin, Eliogarty and the northern parts of Owney and Arra) as well as areas now belonging to the counties of Limerick and Offaly; William de Burgh was granted the western baronies of Clanwilliam and parts of Kilnamanagh Upper and Lower, as well as the south-eastern part of the county (barony of Iffa and Offa East); while Philip of Worcester received the remaining areas of south Tipperary (baronies of Slievardagh, Iffa and Offa West and the southern portion of Middlethird) (Empey 1970, 23-9). Together, these areas represented the eastern half of the former kingdom of Limerick, but this extensive area subsequently proved too difficult to administer properly from Limerick. By the mid-thirteenth century, therefore, it appears that the kingdom was divided into two embryonic counties - those of Limerick and Tipperary (Empey 1981, 16).

Thus, as has been noted by Empey, Tipperary was "something of an artificial creation reflecting the requirements of administrative planners rather than ancient historic boundaries" (1985, 71). This lack of recognition of the old political and ecclesiastical boundaries of the area was probably made possible, in Empey's opinion, by the fact that the Anglo-Norman cantreds of the eastern part of the kingdom of Limerick had already taken firm shape by this time. The cantred was the basic administrative subdivision of the medieval county. Its boundaries frequently coincided with those of the rural deanery - the diocesan subdivision - as well as with those of the great capital manors. The extent of the cantred was, however, based on pre-Norman political and tribal boundaries (*ibid*, 78). The geographical extent of thirteenth-century Tipperary is illustrated in Fig. 4.

In 1329 the county of Tipperary became a liberty under the direct control of James Butler, Earl of Ormond, a descendant of Theobald Walter. This event came about as a result of the disturbed state of the county during the early fourteenth century, and had the effect of extending the Butler lordship over the entire county. The liberty later came to be known as the palatinate of Tipperary, and this continued in existence under the Butlers until as late as 1716.

ANGLO-NORMAN SETTLEMENT

The years between 1185 and 1206 witnessed the disruption and the replacement of the Gaelic order in Tipperary. The Anglo-Norman advance was led by Theobald Walter, William de Burgh and Philip of Worcester. They were principally threatened by Donal More O'Brien of Thomond and Donal MacCarthy of Desmond, but once these were defeated the Irish opposition disintegrated. The county was subsequently divided out among these three Anglo-Norman conquerors, as has been noted above. One obvious consequence of these allocations was that a new feudal regime of landholding, backed up by colonisation, was introduced. Settlers in large numbers arrived from England and Wales and a manorial system was introduced. The organisation of the newly-conquered territories can best be studied by examining the organisation of fourteenth-century manors. Theobald Walter's solution to the problem of administering his huge northern portion of Tipperary, which comprised five cantreds, was to divide the area into four manorial units. Each manor served as the *caput* or capitol of its cantred, fulfilling administrative, tenurial and military functions (Empey 1985, 76-8).

What about the wider social and economic implications of this process of manorialisation and subinfeudation? The quality and extent of demesne lands attached to manors proved that intensive agriculture was regarded as its main priority, with an emphasis on surplus production. While the manorial system varied from region to region and manor to manor, its overall impact on the economy was obviously a dramatic move away from the subsistence agriculture of pre-manorial times. The availability of forests for exploitation, the rich agricultural lands of the Suir basin and the large number of moated sites located on the fringes of manorial lands all attest to the rapidly expanding economy of the thirteenth century (Empey 1985, 81-2).

An inevitable result of the dynamic thirteenth-century changes, which is integrated into Tipperary's modern fabric, was the evolvement of boroughs and towns. The sale of produce in their own markets was an important source of profit for the Anglo-Norman lords. In order to achieve this they had to attract settlers to key areas, and this was achieved by offering them certain rights and privileges as well as land. There was no doubt that some of these boroughs and towns were primarily rooted in agriculture, but some did develop substantial market economies and true urban character.

Bradley defines a medieval town as a "settlement occupying a central position in a communications network, represented by a street pattern with houses and their associated land plots whose density is significantly greater than the settlements immediately around it; it incorporates a market place and a church and its principal functions are reflected by the presence of at least three of the following: town walls, a castle, bridge, cathedral, a house belonging to one of the religious orders, a hospital or leper-house close to the town, an area of specialist technological activity, quays, a large school or administrative building, and/or suburbs" (1985, 35). Under these terms of definition only seven of the minimal total of thirty-five boroughs founded in Tipperary qualify as towns: Carrick-on-Suir, Cashel, Clonmel, Fethard, Nenagh, Thurles and Tipperary. Some boroughs, such as Lisronagh, seem merely to have been farming communities which had the legal advantages of burgage tenure, while others, like Roscrea and Athassel, were more substantial centres (*ibid*, 35-6). As may be seen from Fig.4, the heaviest concentration of both towns and boroughs is on the good agricultural lands east of the river Suir, with Nenagh and Tipperary being the only large towns in the north and west respectively. It would appear, based on the documentary sources, that most of these towns were founded between 1185 and 1230 (*ibid*, 39).

The main architectural features of these towns are: the town wall, defended by gates and mural towers, enclosing a parish church which is invariably located either immediately within the wall, as at Fethard, or in an angle of the wall, as at Clonmel; the street plan which widens at one end to form the market place - a feature which is most striking at Thurles and Fethard; sometimes other structures occur, such as town houses and, of course, various religious houses. The only Dominican foundation was at Cashel, while the Augustinians had friaries at Fethard and Tipperary, the Carmelites at Clonmel and Thurles and the Franciscans at Cashel, Clonmel, Nenagh and Carrick-on-Suir.

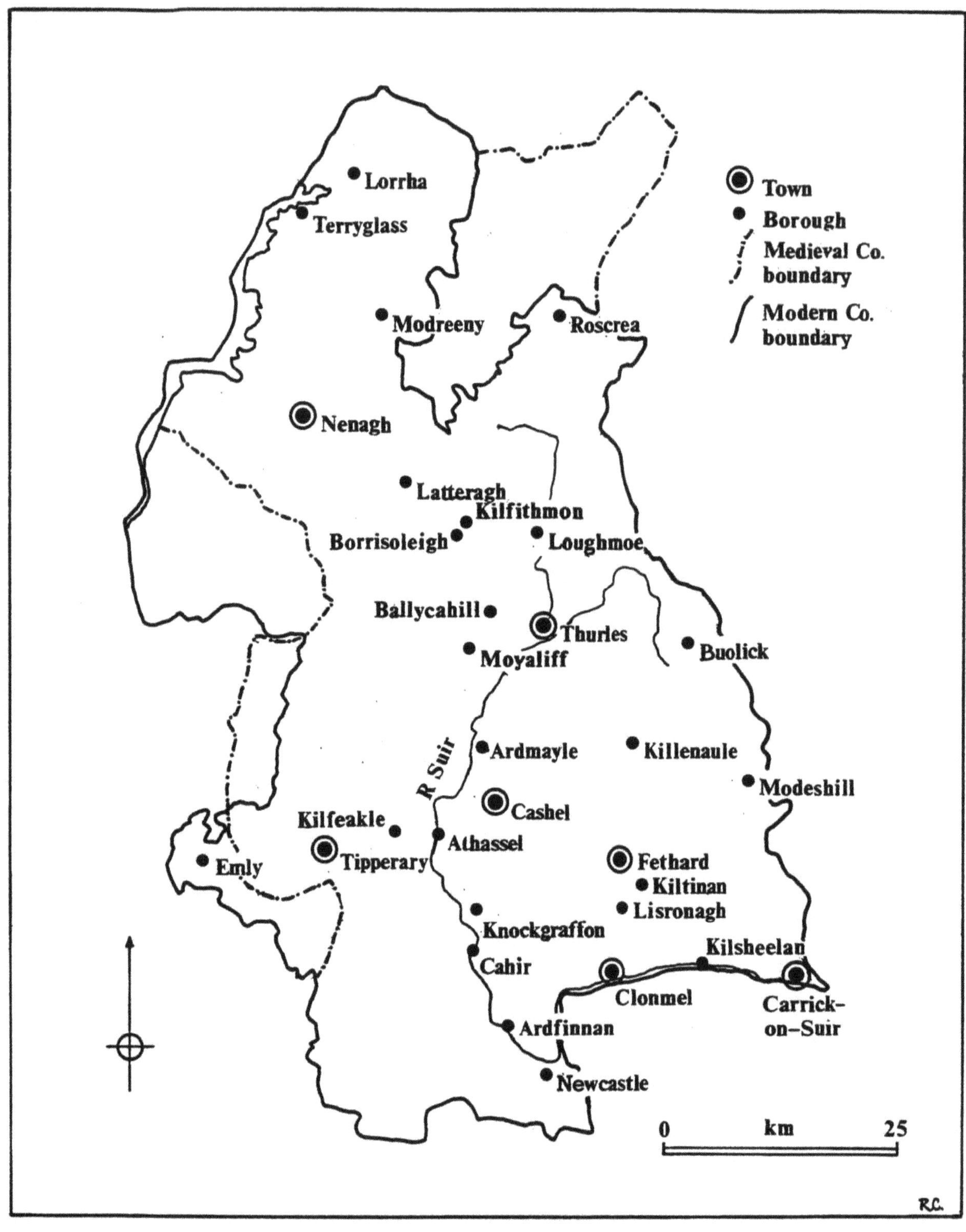

Fig. 4 Map of county Tipperary in the thirteenth century showing location of towns and boroughs (after Bradley 1985 and Empey 1985).

Among the main military monument types introduced by the Anglo-Normans to Ireland are mottes and baileys, ringworks and moated sites (Fig. 5). The motte-and-bailey fortifications were constructed during the initial phase of the Anglo-Norman invasion, primarily as military defenses. At least nine examples occur in Tipperary county and, based on the evidence from excavations elsewhere, their construction dates to the period between 1170 and 1230. Three possible military ringworks have also been identified in the county, all in its north-eastern portion (Stout 1984, 114-16). It is likely, however, that future fieldwork will identify further examples elsewhere in the county.

The moated site is a rectangular earthwork bounded by a bank and an external moat. They are generally dated to the thirteenth and fourteenth centuries, and Tipperary - with a total of 139 examples - has probably the most dense distribution of such sites in Ireland. They probably functioned as the centres of manors. Barry points out how most of the moated sites in Ireland were concentrated in the interface areas between colonists and the indigenous Irish. Tipperary and Wexford, which are on the periphery of the colony, have the densest concentrations, whereas counties located in the heart of the Anglo-Norman area have very small numbers of such sites (1977, 176).

An example of an excavated moated site in Tipperary is Ballyveelish North (Doody 1987, 74-87). No surface traces of it were apparent, but the excavation revealed that it had a large moat and enclosed two partially stone-built houses. The small finds from the Ballyveelish site were typical for medieval rural settlement sites - green glazed sherds of pottery of thirteenth-fourteenth century date, several sherds of thirteenth-century cooking ware, some quernstones, animal bones and pieces of iron nails.

THE GAELIC RESURGENCE

The level of intensity of Anglo-Norman settlement and control in south Tipperary led to the disintegration of the major Gaelic septs there. In the north and north-west of the county, however, where the colonial settlement was relatively weak, the position of the Irish remained strong. While they were undoubtedly forced to yield ground to the colonisers - the Butler overlords - it is also clear that they managed to retain a significant deal of autonomy. Thus Gaelic septs in this area - like the O'Kennedys, the O'Carrolls and the O'Dwyers - developed patron-client relationships with the Butlers but retained the essential features of Gaelic social and political organisation. The principal difference between the north and south of the county was that in the former area the Anglo-Normans did not introduce any significant numbers of settlers and the Irish remained in occupation of the land (Empey 1985, 86-8).

By the beginning of the fourteenth century Anglo-Norman Ireland was undergoing severe economic difficulties. The effects of the Bruce invasion of 1316 were exacerbated by those of the Black Death of 1348. Meanwhile the Tipperary region was under sporadic attack from the Gaelic septs. It was during this period that the Gaelic resurgence began, particularly in the north of the county where the O'Kennedys, the O'Carrolls and the O'Dwyers made significant gains. Coinciding with this type of military activity and the economic downturn the Anglo-Norman society in Tipperary began to gradually adopt Gaelic customs and practices. While this society became more Gaelicised, many facets of the Anglo-Norman landscape and economy nevertheless remained intact into the sixteenth century. The resilience of the market towns is evidence of this (Hennessey 1985, 68), though in overall terms Anglo-Norman settlement had been weakened and modified by the effects of the Gaelic resurgence. In fact, Empey has calculated that the revenues of Nenagh and Thurles fell to about one quarter of their former value in the mid-fourteenth century, a decline from which they never recovered (1985, 89). This poor economic state served to progress the process of Gaelicisation even further, and by the end of this century many Anglo-Norman families, like the Purcells, Bourkes and Hacketts, had become Gaelicised.

Tower houses, characteristic defensive residences of the fourteenth to sixteenth centuries, may be seen as architectural expressions of the cross-fertilisation of the Gaelic and Anglo-Norman cultures. Cairns has shown that there were four hundred and ten definite tower houses in county Tipperary and a possible sixty-three further examples (1987, 3, 5; Fig. 6). They are concentrated in the most fertile areas of the county, especially around Cashel, Fethard and Clonmel, but are also found in large numbers in the Gaelic north. Their is much debate over their function and origin, however, the general consensus being that they evolved to meet specific defensive needs in an economically viable fashion. They mark the shift away from centralised authority in Dublin towards regional power bases, as was exercised by the powerful Anglo-Irish and Gaelic families from the fourteenth century onwards.

THE CHURCH

The Irish early medieval Church was a decentralised monastic one in which the role of the abbot was largely superior to that of the bishop. From the early twelfth century onwards various attempts were made to initiate a fundamental reform of the Church. These attempts included the introduction of continental religious orders, such as those of the Cistercians and Augustinians, to Ireland, as well as the establishment of the basis of a diocesan system of organisation at the synods of Rathbreasail and Kells (Gwynn 1992, 155-92). However, for political and social reasons the efforts of the reform movement to establish a strong episcopacy did not meet with success, not least because of the lack of effective organisation of the secular church at parish level.

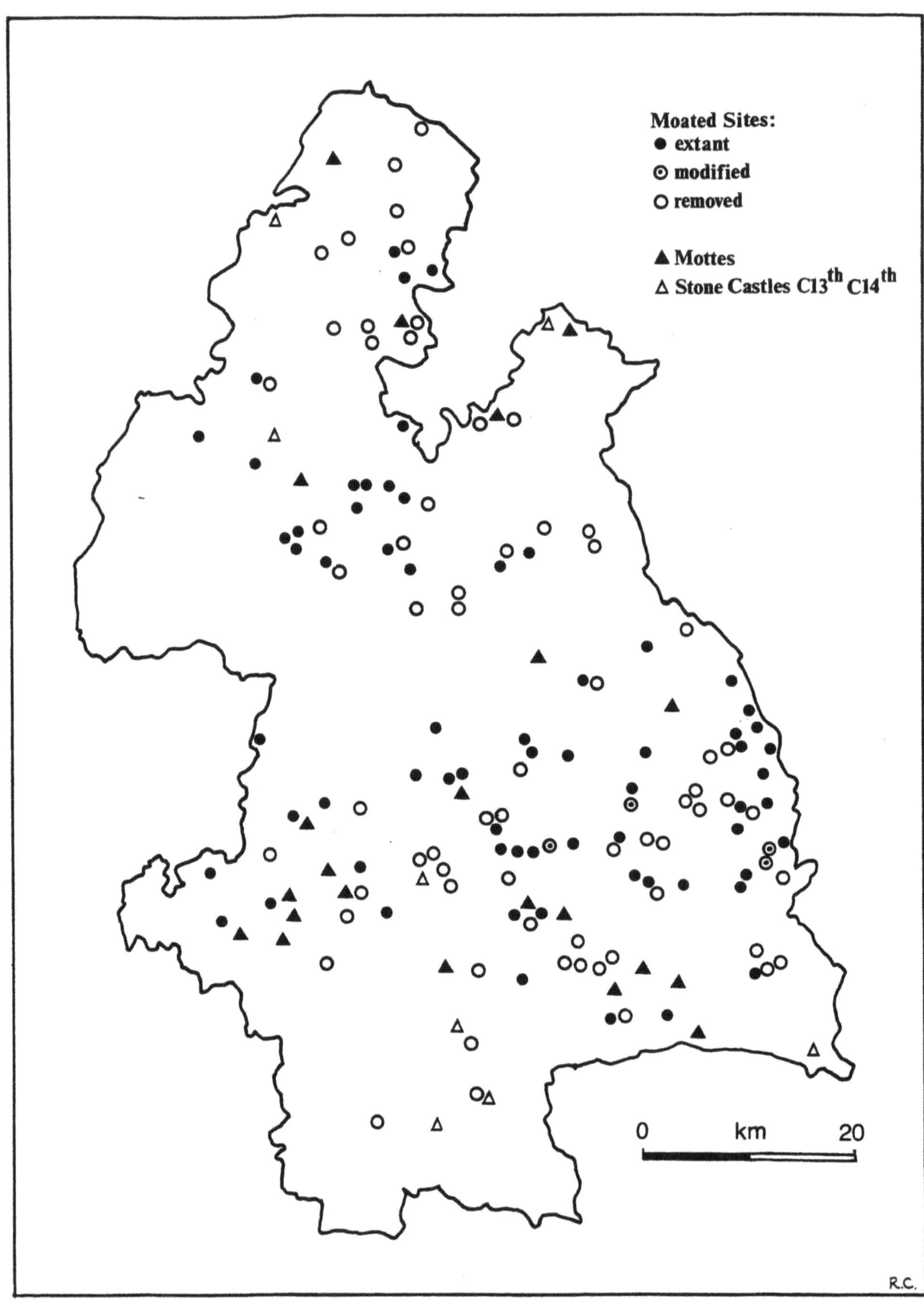

Fig. 5 Distribution of Anglo-Norman fortifications in county Tipperary (after Barry 1977).

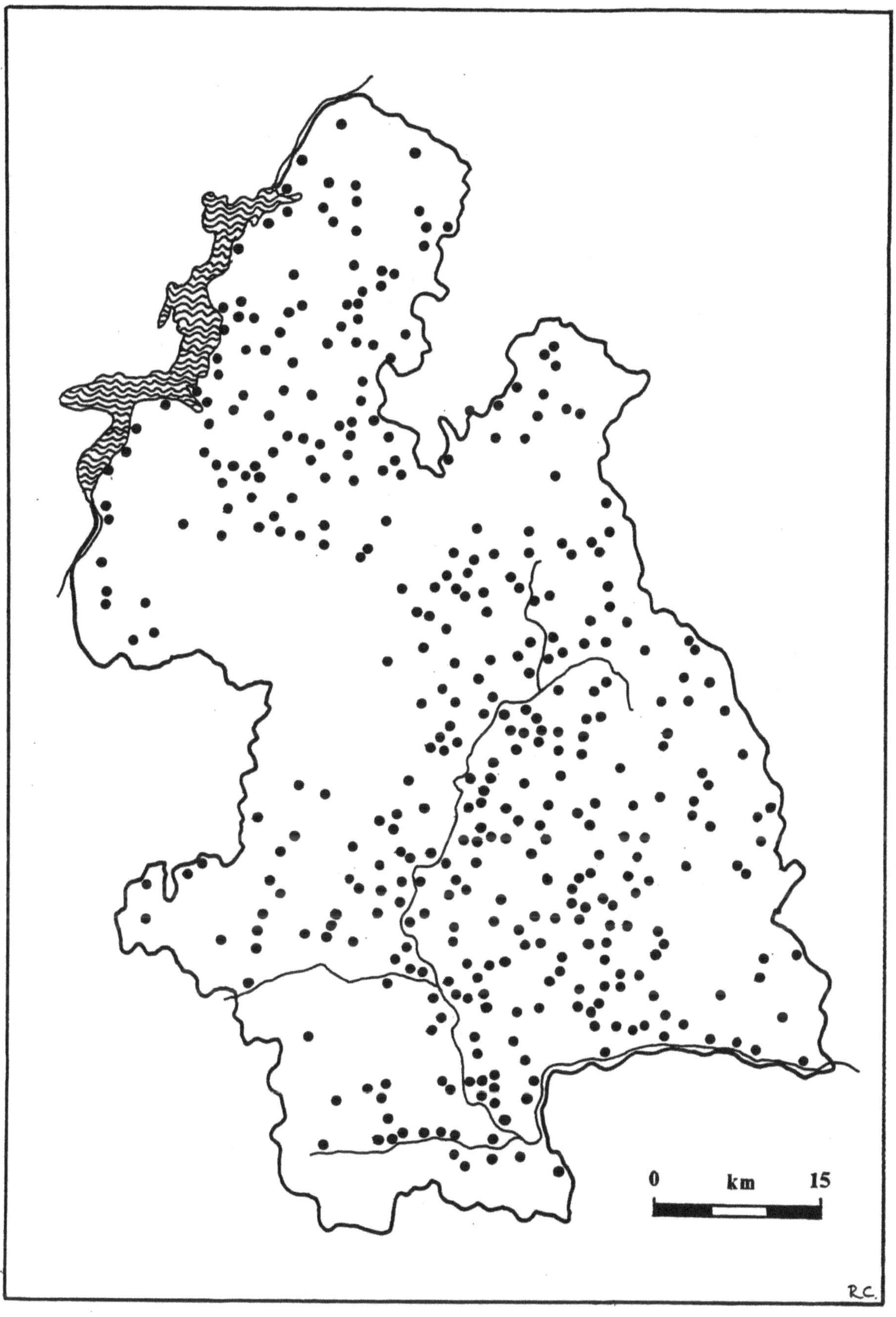

Fig. 6 Distribution of tower houses in county Tipperary (after Cairns 1987).

It was in the area of remodelling the Church at parish level that the Anglo-Normans made their most enduring contribution to the Irish reform. In his consideration of this phenomenon in Tipperary, Hennessey stated "To the Anglo-Norman lords......the introduction of the form of ecclesiastical organisation they were familiar with would have been as essential a part of the colonisation process as the setting up of manors ..... Therefore, once the area later to be known as Tipperary had been successfully conquered and the great magnates had divided out their newly won territories the rapid establishment of a parochial organisation was virtually guaranteed" (1985, 61-62). This task was made all the easier by the collapse of the old Gaelic system, which enabled the Anglo-Normans to proceed with the process of ecclesiastical reorganisation more or less unhindered (and with the support of the crown and the papacy).

The process of parochialisation in Tipperary appears to have begun at the same time as the manorialisation of the county - during the late twelfth and early thirteenth centuries. There was an extremely close territorial relationship between the parish and the manor which, of course, was based on the Gaelic *tuath*. The use of such spatial frameworks clearly facilitated the process of establishing a network of parishes in the county, and it is not surprising that these became fixed earlier in the south where the most intense Anglo-Norman settlement took place (Empey 1985, 84-85; Hennessey 1985, 62-63).

The Gaelic resurgence of the later medieval period did have the effect of contributing towards the disintegration of the ecclesiastical network put in place by the Anglo-Normans. The effectiveness of the system had declined and become highly disorganised by the fifteenth century, when the papal records indicate that many parish churches were in disrepair and that several resident vicars were corrupt or unqualified (Hennessey 1985, 68-70).

Nevertheless, despite these negative later developments, the Anglo-Normans had promoted and introduced a new ecclesiastical system - based on the parish - into Ireland. As Hennessey has pointed out in relation to Tipperary, this was "powerfully symbolised in the landscape by the parish church and the adjacent cemetery" (1985, 70). Together with the medieval monasteries, such as those at Athassel, Kilcooley and Holy Cross, these churches came to be identified as important focal points of identity for the native Irish as well as the descendants of the Anglo-Normans. It is in this context that the medieval grave-slabs that occur in so many of them should be considered.

GRAVE-SLAB GROUPS

The aim of this chapter is to discuss the identifiable groups of grave-slabs within county Tipperary (Fig. 13). The identification and classification of these groups are based primarily on the cross-head designs of the slabs. Where it is possible, similarities are drawn with other Irish and British medieval grave-slabs. After each group is identified, the grave-slabs are discussed. A date is assigned to each of these groups, based on grave-slabs with dated inscriptions, on similarities between undated and dated slabs and on other features.

GROUP 1: TRANSITIONAL SLABS

This is a small group comprising four slabs from Baptist Grange, Coolmundry and Kiltinan. These form a distinct group with no known parallels elsewhere in Ireland. In form, they appear to be transitional between early medieval and Anglo-Norman types of design.

Although the slabs, except for Kiltinan 1 and 2, occur in different townlands, they are still located within a short distance of each other. They also have certain distinct features in common, for example their extreme thickness, the type of stone used and the style of their carving and design. One of the most significant features of slabs in this group is their average thickness, which is nearly twice that of other medieval slabs from Tipperary. Secondly, all four slabs are of sandstone; only seven out of the one hundred and seven slabs in Tipperary are of sandstone, a fact which further underlines the distinctive nature of these Group 1 slabs. None of the slabs feature a chamfer or inscription, though they each display a distinct tapered form. Kiltinan 1 and 2 and Coolmundry 1 feature a grooved frame which extends along the sides and across the top of the slabs. In the case of Baptist Grange 1, a raised frame occurs.

Each slab in this group features a different design, though there are some basic similarities. Firstly, the cross-stem on each of the slabs is formed by three parallel grooves (Fig. 38) and, secondly, the whole design is executed in grooves in all cases, as opposed to being incised or carved in relief. It must be stated, however, that Baptist Grange 1 and Kiltinan 1 and 2 are presently standing upside down with only their lower portions visible.

There is no doubt that Coolmundry 1 stands the right way up as it tapers inwards from head to base. The design it features is of a multi-linear, ringed cross-form. It features a sub-circular cross-head with the remains of three short arms. Its ringed form is related to numerous early medieval cross types. The boxed termination to cross-shafts, as seen on Kiltinan 1, is very common on early medieval slabs in the west of Ireland and is seen, for instance, at Iniscealtra, Co. Clare, Inishmore, Co. Galway and Inishmurray, Co. Sligo. The design at the base of the cross-stem of Kiltinan 2 consists of a rectangular pedestal-like feature which terminates in a pair of simple volutes. This form occurs in a number of medieval contexts - most notably on some of the Kilfenora high crosses (de Paor 1956, 58-59) - although comparisons may also be made with volute features which occur on some early medieval cross-slabs, for example from Clonmacnoise, Co. Offaly (Macalister 1909, no. 98).

A twelfth-thirteenth century date is suggested for this small but interesting group of Tipperary slabs which, it is suggested, forms a type which is transitional between native early medieval and introduced Anglo-Norman types. This proposed date is based on the Clare and Aran parallels and on the early medieval cross-head forms. Other features support this proposed dating. The slabs taper distinctly, for instance, and this is a feature of other types of twelfth-thirteenth century slabs. One cannot conclude without doubt that the use of sandstone was exclusively a twelfth-thirteenth century phenomenon, however, though it was commonly used for fittings in ecclesiastical architecture during this period. The third feature which points to an early date is the design, which is basic both in terms of its form and style of carving.

The similarities between these four slabs in the choice of stone, the overall nature of the design, their distinct taper and their close geographical proximity all point to their belonging to a definite group. They were possibly carved by the same person, who was probably of local origin and free from most Anglo-Norman influences.

GROUP 2: HEAD-SLABS

The classic head-slab can be defined as a tapered slab which features a human head carved in high relief above a floriated cross. There are just over thirty examples known in Ireland. While the majority are tapered, rectangular forms are also known, as, for example, from Trim, Co. Meath (Hunt 1974, cat. 209). Even though most of the slabs feature heads carved in relief, incised examples are also known. These latter include those from Jerpoint, Co. Kilkenny, and Tullylease, Co. Cork (*ibid*, cat. 116 and 13a). Examples also occur in which the head is set within a sunken reserve, as, for example, at Gowran, Co. Kilkenny and St. Canice's, Kilkenny (*ibid*, cat. 101 and 134). The other main attribute of these slabs is the floriated cross, which can occur in incised or relief form. The example in St. Patrick's Cathedral, Cashel, for example, bears an incised cross (*ibid*, cat. 235) whereas that in New Ross, Co. Wexford, is in relief

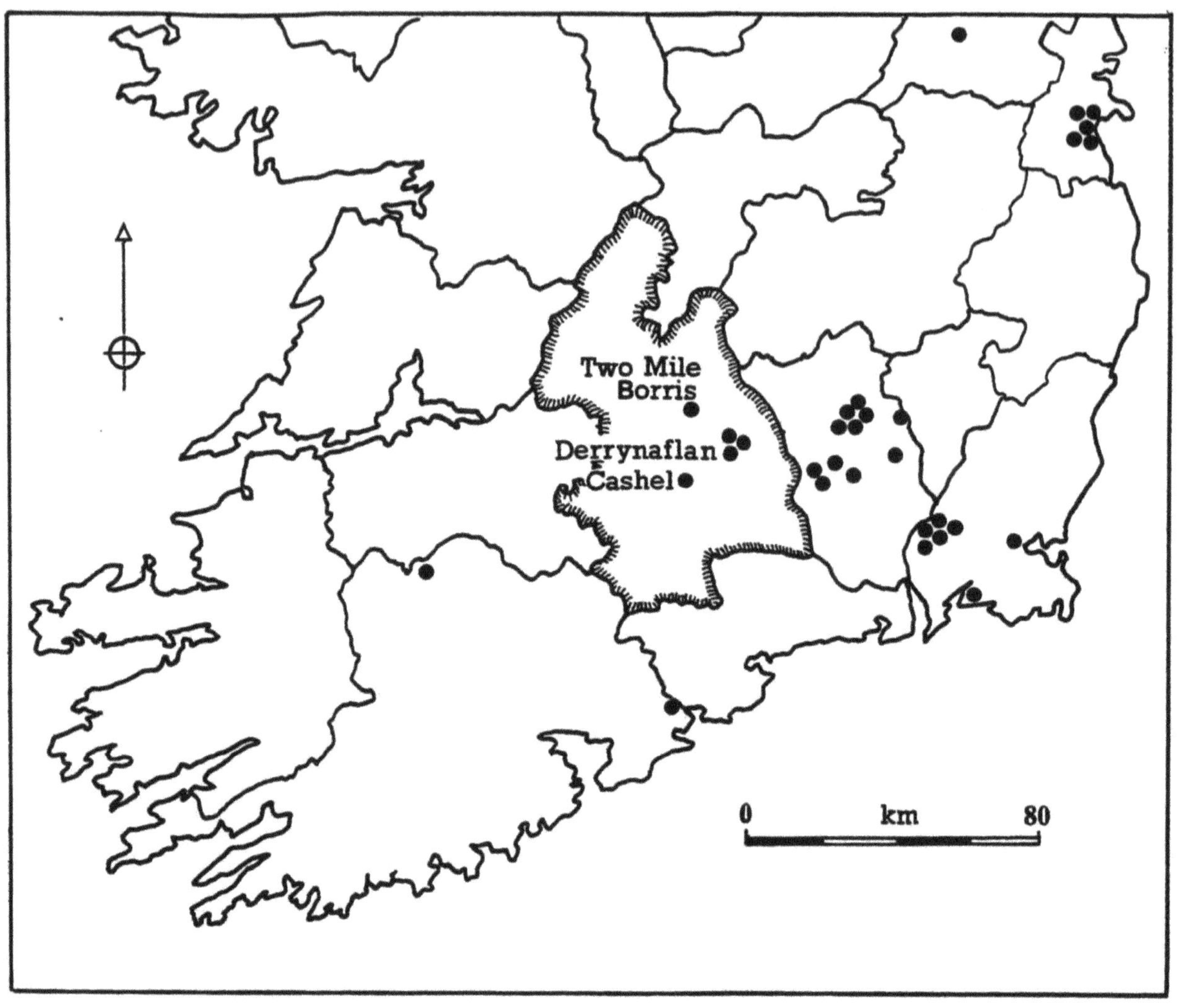

Fig. 7 Distribution of head-slabs in Ireland (after Maher 1994).

(*ibid*, cat. 101). While most of the slabs bear the same type of floriated cross, three of them feature a 'bracelet' cross-form. This is a cross formed from four penannular circles and can be dated to the thirteenth century in Britain (Ryder 1985, 9-10). Examples of this cross-type also occur in Christchurch, Dublin and St. Mary's Church, New Ross, Co. Wexford (*ibid*, cat. 29, 30 and 269).

The main concentration of head-slabs in Ireland is in the south-east (Fig. 7). There is one example each in counties Kerry, Cork and Meath, and a few examples occur in Dublin. All Irish head-slabs seem to date to the thirteenth and early fourteenth centuries (Hunt 1974, 41). Given the general form of these slabs, that is their tapered aspect and the type of cross they feature, such a date range is not surprising. Details other than the form of the slabs themselves also point towards such a date. The hair-style and head-dresses on the carved heads are of particular importance in this regard. The style of head-dress on the civilian ladies' slabs is invariably a pill-box with barbette, as seen, for example, on the slab at Black Abbey, Co. Kilkenny (*ibid*, cat. 130). In the case of the civilian male head-slabs, the typical thirteenth to fourteenth century style is the hair curling outwards below the ears, as seen for example on the slab from Cashel, (*ibid*, cat. 235). Only a minority of the slabs bear inscriptions but these, significantly, occur in Lombardic lettering. This can also be used as a basis for placing the slabs within the above stated date range.

Hunt divides head-slabs into three categories - those of civilian ladies, civilian males and ecclesiastics. Also aligned to this group are the double head-slabs. The civilian ladies' head-slabs served as the memorials for the wives of the merchant class (*ibid*, 37). The head-dresses carved on these slabs are typical of the thirteenth to early fourteenth centuries. They feature open-topped 'pill-box' hats with a barbette - a piece of folded linen which passes twice around the face and under the chin. The ends are pinned on top of the head. There are exact parallels for this head-dress type on two corbels from the lady chapel in Kilkenny (*ibid*, 36), of which the construction may be dated to *c*. 1280 (Leask 1960, 110).

The typical hair-style depicted on the civilian male slabs involves the hair extending to the ears in a chevelure curling, as seen, for example, on a slab from Black Abbey, Kilkenny (Hunt 1974, cat. 135). Hunt suggests that this hair-style can be dated to shortly after 1300 (*ibid*, 184). There are only three ecclesiastical head-slabs, all located in Co. Kilkenny. A feature that these slabs have in common is the orle of hair, which rings around the temple and head. This orle-like band is most clearly seen on the head-slab at St. Canice's Cathedral, Kilkenny (*ibid*, cat. 134).

Of the fourth group - the double head-slabs - there are only four recorded examples, one each in counties Kilkenny, Wexford, Dublin and Meath. A previously unrecorded example occurs at Derrynaflan (Maher 1994, 162-66). These slabs feature two carved human heads, one of a male and the other of a female. The hair-style and head-dress depicted follow the same conventions as are found on other head-slabs, and the double head-slabs also feature a cross. Both the floriated type and the 'bracelet' cross-form are found associated with this group. The double head-slab at Trim, Co. Meath, also features a crucifixion scene (Hunt 1974, cat. 209).

Hunt records only two head-slabs from county Tipperary - one at Two-Mile-Borris old village cemetery (*ibid*, cat. 249) and one at St. Patrick's Cathedral, Cashel, which was originally located at the Presentation Convent, Cashel (*ibid*, cat. 235). This total may now be increased to five with the recognition of a group of three at Derrynaflan monastic site (Maher 1994). The Cashel example conforms to the classic head-slab type, but unfortunately its Lombardic inscription is totally unintelligible. The slabs at Derrynaflan and Two-Mile-Borris all deviate from the classic form. Derrynaflan 2 features the remains of a carved head in relief, but no other apparent design, while Derrynaflan 1 and 3 each feature a somewhat unusual design.

Derrynaflan 1 (Fig. 8) features a carved human head in relief. Unfortunately, its upper portion is defaced and only the base of the nose, the mouth and the neck survive. What may be crude representations of feet are carved in relief at the base of the slab. An incised design begins at the base of the head and terminates at the top of the feet. The top of the design consists of an incised circle which encloses a cross formed from the juxtapositioning of four penannular circles. At the centre of the composition is a lozenge. The vertical arm terminals do not survive, but it is likely that similar designs occurred here. This cruciform design is not unlike Ryder's 'bracelet' cross-form (1985, 9-10), which occurs on the head-slabs at St. Mary's Church, New Ross, Co. Wexford and on the two examples at Christchurch, Dublin (Hunt 1974, cat. 97, 99 and 105). Two single stems with lobed terminals extend upwards from the enclosing circle. Between the dexter stem and the carved head a circular design is formed from four lentoids disposed around a small circle. An incised human head is linked to the base of the enclosing circle by a pair of small grooves; the former features eyes, a nose and a mouth. A double outline central shaft extends from the base of the incised human head to the carved 'feet'. Two smaller stems extend out, upwardly disposed from this central shaft, and end in lobed terminals. Two similar stems extend from its base. Even though the basic cruciform design can be paralleled with other head-slabs, the overall design of this slab is not comparable.

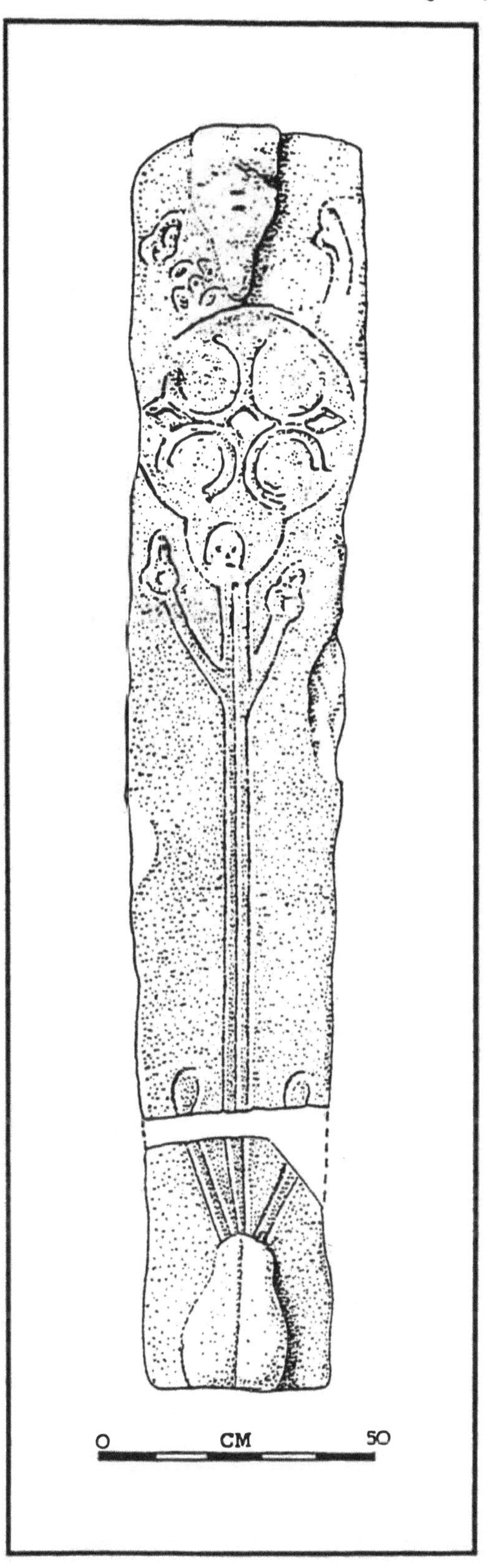

Fig. 8 Slab No. 1, Derrynaflan.

Derrynaflan 3, which survives in two portions, features two carved human heads both of which are defaced. The only surviving features of the head on the dexter side are the mouth and the neck. No features survive on the other head. A motif carved in relief, consisting of four lentoids in a circle, occurs between the two carved heads. Beneath the two heads are the remains of two poorly preserved incised crosses. These are contained within outline circles which surmount narrow cross-stems, which only partly survive. The crosses are formed from the juxtapositioning of four penannular circles, which results in a cross with expanded terminals and hollowed angles.

Even though the designs on Derrynaflan 1 and 3 deviate somewhat from the classic head-slab design, it is possible to argue that they are contemporary. The basis for such an argument lies in the general form of the Derrynaflan slabs - they are all tapered and they bear simple incised designs which are characteristic of later slabs. The cruciform design of Derrynaflan 1, which is related to the 'bracelet' cross-form of other head-slabs, points, perhaps, to a thirteenth-century date.

However, one can more convincingly argue for a fourteenth- to fifteenth-century date for these slabs. Even though Derrynaflan 1 and 3 bear features comparable to the 'classic' head-slab, they appear to belong to a more degenerate group, featuring a combination of non-native and native influences. The latter manifest themselves in the form of the motif composed of lentoids on slab no. 1 and in the close similarities between the cross-forms of Derrynaflan 3 and some cross-slabs of the early medieval period. The poor quality of the stone, along with the plain human heads, also point to the Derrynaflan slabs as being outside the 'classic' head-slab group.

The most unusual feature of the head-slab at Two-Mile-Borris is its pointed top. However, the floriated cross and the human head, both carved in relief, follow the 'classic' head-slab style. The number of medieval slabs which feature a pointed top is limited. One example occurs at St. Canice's Cathedral, Kilkenny, which Bradley dates to the thirteenth or fourteenth century (1985, cat. 23), while another occurs on the site of the churchyard of St. Peter's, West Out, Lewis, Sussex. It is dated to the thirteenth century (Styan 1902, pl. LXII). A third example exists in the cathedral of Newtown Trim, Co. Meath; here the pointed top is a feature of a carved effigy, dating to the early thirteenth century (Hunt 1974, cat. 197).

The pointed top of the Two-Mile-Borris slab is a unique feature amongst the corpus of Irish head-slabs. However, it does occur on other medieval sepulchral monuments, though not extensively. The parallels all point to a thirteenth-to fourteenth-century date, which conforms with the suggested date range for head-slabs.

The distribution of effigies in Ireland, though somewhat more extensive than that of head-slabs, exhibits the same south-eastern pattern. It could be suggested that the form of incised effigies may have influenced the form of some head-slabs, given that some of the latter exhibit incised heads. On the incised slab at Athassel, Co. Tipperary (Hunt 1974, cat. 222), for instance, there are two features which can be paralleled with the head-slabs. The first of these is the floriated cross which rests on the staff held by the woman, while the second is the hair-style of the man, which curls below the ears. Both features (the former without the staff) are common occurrences on the head-slabs. Further connections between the incised effigies and the incised head-slabs are likely to be found.

GROUP 3: THE SIMPLE FLORIATED CROSS

The typical grave-slab of this type may be described as a tapered slab, with chamfered edges, which features a simple incised floriated cross. A good example of this type is slab no. 2 from the Dominican Abbey, Kilkenny (Prim 1851, 454). Where an inscription occurs on such slabs it is invariably in Lombardic lettering. Variations of the above features, however, can occur: for example, a lozenge-shaped centre may occur instead of a plain centred cross-head as is the case on a slab in St. Canice's Cathedral, Kilkenny (Bradley 1985, cat. no. 2, fig. 3). Secondly, additional features may occur along the cross-shaft: for example a knop or cross-band may occur at the base of the cross-head or along the cross-shaft, as, for example, on a slab in St. Mary's Churchyard, New Ross, Co. Wexford (Vigors 1898, 501). The terminals of these cross-shafts quite often take the form of a single fleur-de-lis or trefoil, though examples do occur where the base is stepped. The stepped base became more common in the late fourteenth century and was eventually replaced by the pillar-base form. Despite such variations, the basic form of the crosses in this group is essentially the same.

A characteristic attribute of these slabs is their distinct taper. Even though grave-slabs from the succeeding centuries are sometimes tapered, the taper is not as pronounced as on the earlier slabs. The same may also be said of the chamfer. In most cases the earlier slabs feature a chamfer, along all four edges, which is wider and more distinct than those on the later examples. As with the cross form, variation in the latter two features - most notably with regard to scale - can also occur. However, when all factors are taken into account - style, form and design - these slabs clearly stand out as a distinct group.

Whilst considering the form and style of this group and its relationship to later types, it is important to take into consideration their original function and positions. In the thirteenth and fourteenth centuries burial in slab-lined graves was a common practice (Bradley 1988, 74). Another form of burial, however, involved the use of a stone coffin or sarcophagus. This was not as common as the slab-lined grave, with only seventeen examples of such

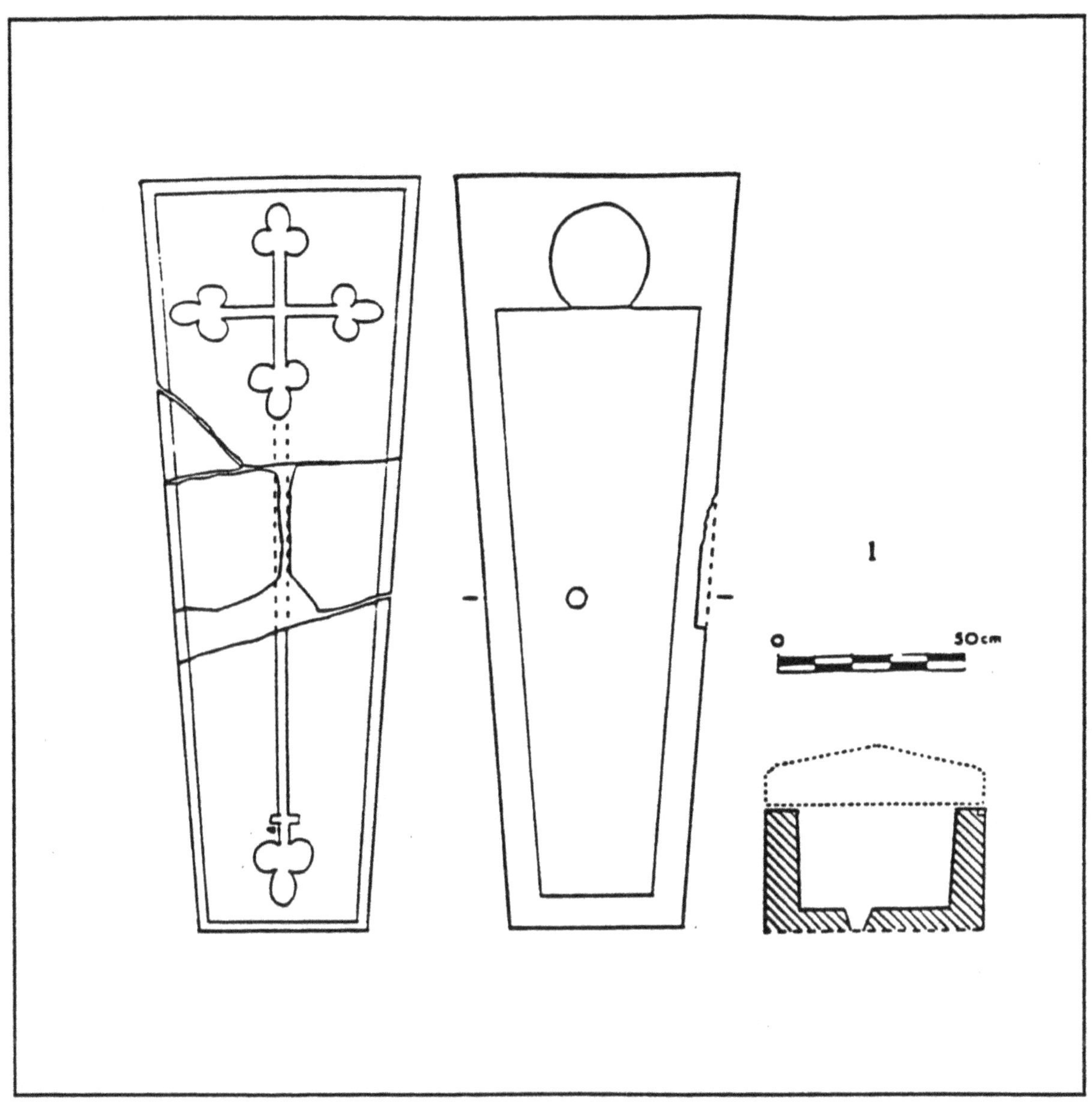

Fig. 9 Thirteenth century sarcophagus lid, Bannow church, county Wexford (after Bradley 1988).

coffins extant in the country (Bradley 1988, 74). It is highly probable that many, if not all, of Group 3 slabs were in fact 'coffin lids' designed to lie on top of the slab-lined graves, or, more probably, to serve as lids for sarcophagi. In St. Mary's church, Bannow, Co. Wexford, for example (Fig. 9), a tomb-slab is cemented onto a plinth beside a sarcophagus which Bradley claims to be its original lid (1988, 79). This grave-slab bears all the characteristics of the group under discussion: it is of tapered form, with four chamfered edges, and features an incised floriated cross, terminating in a cross-band, surmounting a single fleur-de-lis. The slab-lined graves and sarcophagi were very often of trapezoidal plan, such as the slab-lined grave at Swords Castle, Dublin (Fanning 1975, 60), a shape reflected in the form of the grave-slabs. There is no reason to doubt that other such slabs might also have served this purpose.

Overall it can be said that these slabs were placed in recumbent positions and acted as lids for some form of trapezoidal grave - probably a slab-lined grave or sarcophagus. All of these slabs, however, now occur in secondary positions: some stand upright in graveyards while others lie in the ruins of medieval abbeys or act as paving slabs in churches. In the following centuries the distinct 'coffin-shaped' or tapered slabs were replaced by tomb stereotypes, resulting in more rectangular forms of greater dimensions and more elaborate designs.

Unfortunately, very few of the Group 3-type slabs are dated. The two slabs that provide unequivocal dates both occur in Kilkenny: the first is from St. Canice's Cathedral and is a tapered slab with chamfered edges which features an incised floriated cross (with a lozenge-shaped centre) and a

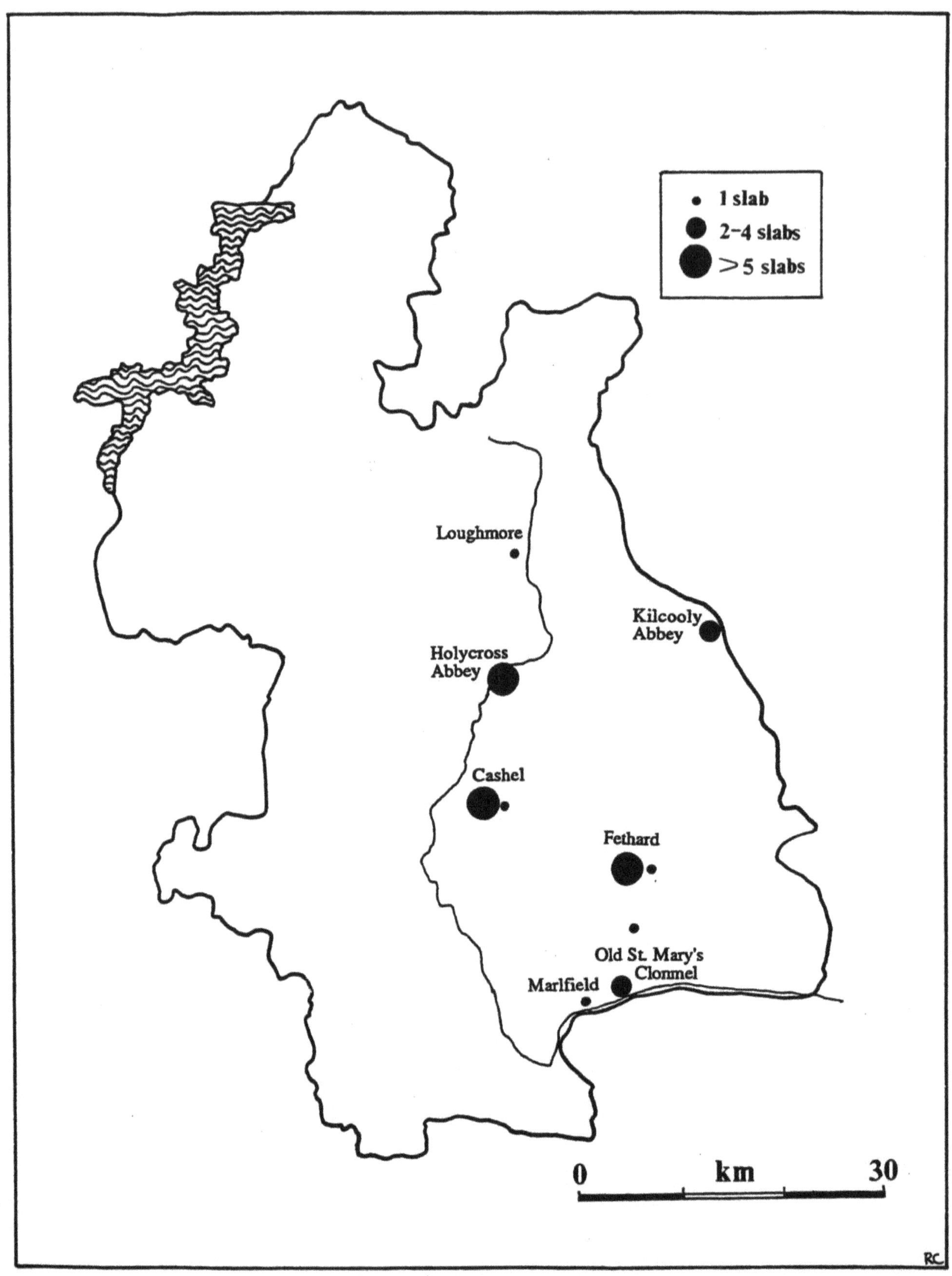

Fig. 10 Distribution of Group 4 grave-slabs in county Tipperary.

Lombardic inscription which provides the date 128(5x8) (Bradley 1985, cat. no. 2, fig. 3); the second example is the Keteller stone, which is also a tapered slab featuring an incised outline floriated cross and a lozenge-shaped centre (Vigors 1895, 79-81) - its Lombardic inscription occurs along the two sides and across the top and provides the date 1280. The majority of Group 3 slabs have been generally dated to the thirteenth or fourteenth centuries, based on comparisons with similar dated slabs and on general design and form. In St. Mary's Church, New Ross, for example, a tapered slab bearing a Lombardic inscription in Norman-French does not provide an exact date, though such inscriptions, especially in Norman French, abounded in England during the latter end of the thirteenth century (Vigors 1900, 501).

The design and form of these slabs may also be generally paralleled with certain features of the Group 2 head-slabs. Shared characteristics include their tapered aspect and the design of the cross, which is usually of simple, incised, floriated form (however, crosses in relief also occur). As stated already, such head-slabs can also date to the thirteenth and fourteenth centuries. Even though they form a group of their own, because of the carved human head they bear, their tapered form and the cross design can be used as another basis for dating the Group 3 slabs.

Slabs similar to the Group 3 Tipperary examples occur in England where they, too, are dated to the thirteenth or fourteenth centuries. In the Durham collection, however, additional features, such as the sunken cross-head and various symbols (for example, the sword), occur very commonly (Ryder 1985, 15-40). Ryder sees these slabs as derivatives of his thirteenth-century 'Bracelet-cross form' (1985, 11), indicating another basis from which these slabs may be dated. Other parallels in England include those published by Styan, one such example being from the Guildhall Museum, London. It consists of the upper portion of a tapered slab, with a double chamfer, which features a Lombardic inscription and a floriated cross. Styan dates this to the thirteenth century (1902, 30). A second such example occurs in Hemsby churchyard, Norfolk. This tapered slab bears a floriated cross, terminating in a stepped base. Styan also dates this slab to the thirteenth century (*ibid*, 42).

No dated example of a Group 3 slab occurs in Tipperary. Overall this slab type is poorly represented in the county, however, with only ten slabs falling into this category: Holycross 5 and 10, Fethard Holy Trinity Church 2, 3, 4 and 5, (Figs. 32, 33), Athassel Abbey 3, 5 and 7 and Marlfield 1. Five of these consist of the lower portion of a tapered slab featuring the remains of incised cross-shafts which terminate in trefoils. Holycross 10, Marlfield 1 and Fethard Holy Trinity Church 3 are complete slabs, all featuring simple floriated crosses, while Fethard Holy Trinity Church 4 and 5 consist of portions of tapered slabs featuring incised cross-shafts terminating in stepped bases. Holycross 2, 3 and 4, which do not feature designs or inscriptions, but are tapered and chamfered, could also possibly be placed in this group. Perhaps they served the same purpose, but were of lesser social significance.

These slabs appear to be more numerous in counties Wexford, Kilkenny and Cork. This is not surprising as this is the area which was first subjected to Norman influences. Not surprisingly, this distribution also overlaps with that of extant stone sarcophagi (Bradley 1988, fig. 1). The distribution pattern advanced here is based mainly on bibliographic research and, no doubt, with more extensive fieldwork, will be expanded in the future. For example a grave-slab set in the floor of the sacristy of Ennis friary, Co. Clare, possibly fits into this category. It is tapered and features the lower half of an incised cross-shaft, terminating in a stepped base. Unfortunately the upper portion of the design is not visible.

GROUP 4: THE SEVEN-ARMED CROSS

The most common medieval grave-slab type in county Tipperary is the rectangular slab featuring a seven-armed floriated cross (Fig. 10). All such slabs appear to have functioned as tomb lids. Their principal attributes include a rectangular form (though some tapered examples are known) and a seven-armed cross - invariably carved in relief - which terminates in a pillar-base form. One exception is Loughmore 1, where the cross-head is carved in low relief but surmounts an incised outline shaft. Another common attribute of these slabs is the raised border which occurs along their sides, top and base, on which a Black Letter inscription is usually carved. This type of grave-slab is the most elaborate of all, displaying a strong sense of permanence and power, and dates to the sixteenth and early seventeenth centuries.

It would not be inconsistent with the evidence to suggest that the majority of these slabs functioned as tomb lids, especially when a number of *in situ* tomb lids provide exact parallels for them, as, for example, Holycross 9. An upright position for such slabs is out of the question when one takes their size into consideration. Therefore a recumbent position as a floor-slab or tomb lid was more likely. Within this group a number of slabs have certain features which point to the latter function as being the more common. For example, the disposition of the lettering on Fethard Abbey 5 makes it clear that the inscription was meant to be read from one side only. In addition, a moulding - which occurs along the sinister edge, across the top and probably along the base (which is presently below ground level) - clearly indicates that this slab formed the lid of a tomb which was designed to be set against a wall. Fethard Abbey 4 which features multiple moulding on the sinister edge only, may also have served as the lid of a tomb set against a wall or in a tomb niche. The sinister edge of Fethard Abbey 6 features an undercut chamfer, the other three edges being straight-cut, indicating that this too functioned as a tomb lid.

The seven-armed, floriated, segmented cross-head terminating in a pillar-base form, with one or more cross-bands occurring at the base of the cross-head and cross-shaft, was a standard design among these sixteenth and early seventeenth century grave-slabs. However, variations to the base and cross-head can occur, with some of the pillar-base forms being quite elaborate. An example of one such base is Fethard Abbey 9 (Fig. 28), but others are of more simple form, for example Cashel 21. The tiered base is also quite common, occurring, for example, on slabs at Knocktopher Abbey, Co. Kilkenny (Langrishe 1905, 365) and St. Patrick's Cathedral, Cashel 3. There are also a number of Group 4 slabs which feature stepped bases, though these are not as common as the pillar-base form. Examples of slabs with this feature include St. Patrick's Cathedral, Cashel 20 and 14.

In the Tipperary group little or no variation is evident in the basic form of the cross-head, except for variation in the floriated arm terminals. However, outside of the Tipperary group another form of seven-armed cross-head is known - the seven armed, interlaced, and/or ringed, cross. Several examples of this type occur at St. Canice's Cathedral, Kilkenny (Bradley 1985, no. 54, fig. 37, no. 57, fig. 40, no. 60, fig. 41, and no. 81, fig. 56), while the Hurley slab in Waterford and the slab of Robert Walsh and Katherine Power at Jerpoint Abbey, Co. Kilkenny, also feature this distinctive style of cross-head. All the above-mentioned examples date to the sixteenth century.

Most Group 4 slabs from Tipperary carry inscriptions, many of which contain interesting information. In some cases there is proof that the monuments were commissioned before the actual death of the person commemorated occurred: for example the inscription on Fethard Abbey 11. There is also an example of a slab in St. Mary's Church, New Ross, Co. Wexford (Garstin 1899, 321), which was commissioned years after the death of the individual. Its inscription reads:

> Here lies Peter Butler, son of Richard, Lord Viscount of Mountgarret, formerly of Cloaghnekyrach, Esquire, who died on the 4th day of June A.D. 1599, and his wife Margaret Devereux who caused this monument to be made in the month of December A.D. 1609, and departed from this world...

In other cases it is unclear what the date on the slab refers to - is it the date of death or the date of commission of the monument? The translation of the inscription on Fethard Abbey 11, for example, reads:

> Here lies Thadeus Owns Meagher and Honora Keeghan, his wife, who erected this monument before their death A.D. 1540.

In this case 1540 could either refer to their date of death or the date of commission of the monument. To commission a monument before death has important social implications, and to find evidence for this gives us insight into society in medieval times. This point will be discussed further in Chapter 7.

There are four examples of Group 4 slabs of banded cross-shaft form, that is they feature an interlocked pair of rectangular forms, open at the base, which occupy the central part of the slab. The four examples - St. Patrick's Cathedral, Cashel 2 and 3 Kilcooley 2 and Holycross 7 - also have other features which serve to link them as a group: firstly, the way in which the fleurs-de-lis penetrate the raised border which carries the inscription; secondly, the style of the fleurs-de-lis is very similar, and thirdly, each of the slabs share rather elaborate 'H' forms at the beginning of each inscription. There is, however, some variation on the type of cross-base represented on these four examples, but the overall impression is that they are closely related and probably represent the work of one carver. Each of the four slabs comes from a major site - a cathedral or large monastic site - where an important craftsman would have been likely to secure patronage.

Three of the Tipperary Group 4 slabs of banded cross-shaft type date to the sixteenth century, with St. Patrick's Cathedral, Cashel 3 being undated. Examples of this type also occur outside of Tipperary, including St. Canice's Cathedral, Kilkenny (Bradley 1985, cat. no. 34, fig. 25, cat. no. 81, fig. 56, and cat. no. 57, fig. 40), Kilree, Co. Kilkenny (Anon 1901, 86), 'French Church' ruins, Waterford (Vigors 1907, 190) and St. Mary's Church, New Ross, which has four slabs bearing this feature (*ibid* 1899, 321, 328; 1900, 500) and (*ibid* 1896, 353). All of these examples also date to the sixteenth century, with the exception of one example at New Ross which dates to 1609 (*ibid* 1899, 321). They are all of rectangular shape, featuring a seven-armed cross and a Black Letter inscription. The banded cross-shaft feature appears to have been widespread, therefore, and not confined to any one particular area.

Another ancillary feature of some Group 4 slabs is the presence of additional designs in the four segments of the cross-head. This feature is rare, with only four recorded examples in Tipperary. In each case they occur on cross-heads of Group 4 type. Three examples occur at Fethard Abbey (no's 10, 11 and 2 Fig. 29) and one at Lisronagh, (no. 1, Fig. 11). The designs consist of foliate and petalled forms, though some are indecipherable. In the case of Lisronagh 1 some of the designs are of Celtic form. The nature of this slab, however, is different from that of the three examples in Fethard Abbey in that it displays strong Celtic affinities (Maher 1992, 30-37). The three examples in Fethard Abbey, on the other hand, were probably the work of one carver as they share certain features. These include the form of the cross-arm terminals, the similarities of the motifs occupying the sunken segments of each of the cross-heads and the presence of heraldic shields on two of the slabs.

The presence of heraldic shields and motifs is not a very common feature of medieval grave-slabs. However, a number of examples occur around the country. Whilst they mainly occur on the elaborate sixteenth and seventeenth century grave-slabs, earlier examples are also known; for example the De Clare tombstone in Kells Abbey, Co. Kilkenny, which probably dates to the thirteenth or fourteenth century (Anon 1898, 82). There are only five instances of slabs in this corpus bearing heraldic shields, all of Group 4 type: Fethard Abbey 2, 3 and 11, Old St. Mary's, Clonmel 1, and St. Patrick's, Cashel 15. Examples outside of Tipperary occur in counties Meath, Kilkenny and Wexford, and date to between 1501 and 1637. Heraldry serves the purpose of both enhancing the impressiveness of the grave-slabs and drawing attention to the social significance of the people commemorated by them. The only passion symbol to occur on the Group 4 Tipperary slabs is the skull and cross-bones. In fact, in this catalogue there is only one example of its occurrence, that is Old St. Mary's 2. This slab features a seven-armed cross with fleur-de-lis terminals and a simple pillar-base form, which features a skull and cross-bones. Beneath the base of the cross are inscribed the words *Memento Mori* (Remember Death!). This symbol also occurs on three seventeenth century slabs at Loughmore (Fitzgerald 1902, 258-61). There are no other passion symbols represented Group 4 slabs in Tipperary. However, a few seventeenth-century grave-slabs also feature such symbols; for example Holy Trinity Church, Fethard, and the Catholic graveyard at Lorrha (O'Farrell 1980, 63). Overall the symbols of the passion were not in common usage when the slabs under discussion here were carved.

To sum up, the Group 4 slabs feature a standard seven-armed, segmented cross, terminating in a pillar-base form. A raised border occurs around the slab and may or may not feature a Black Letter inscription. It is quite possible, based on chamfer details, inscription layout, etc., that a large number of these slabs served as tomb lids, and are now in secondary positions. This type of slab is the most elaborate of the Tipperary types, and a range of ancillary motifs and symbols may occur on it.

GROUP 5: MISCELLANEOUS SLABS

The slabs which constitute this group comprise a series which exhibit none of the cross-forms outlined for the above groups. They are found at a number of individual locations in Tipperary (Fig. 12), at some of which slabs of the other groups are also represented. These slabs range in date throughout the medieval period. In this section they are dealt with according to the sites which they are found in, as there are clear indications that the slabs from some sites are related to one another in style. Nonetheless, none of these constitute discrete groups for they do not exhibit similar cross-forms.

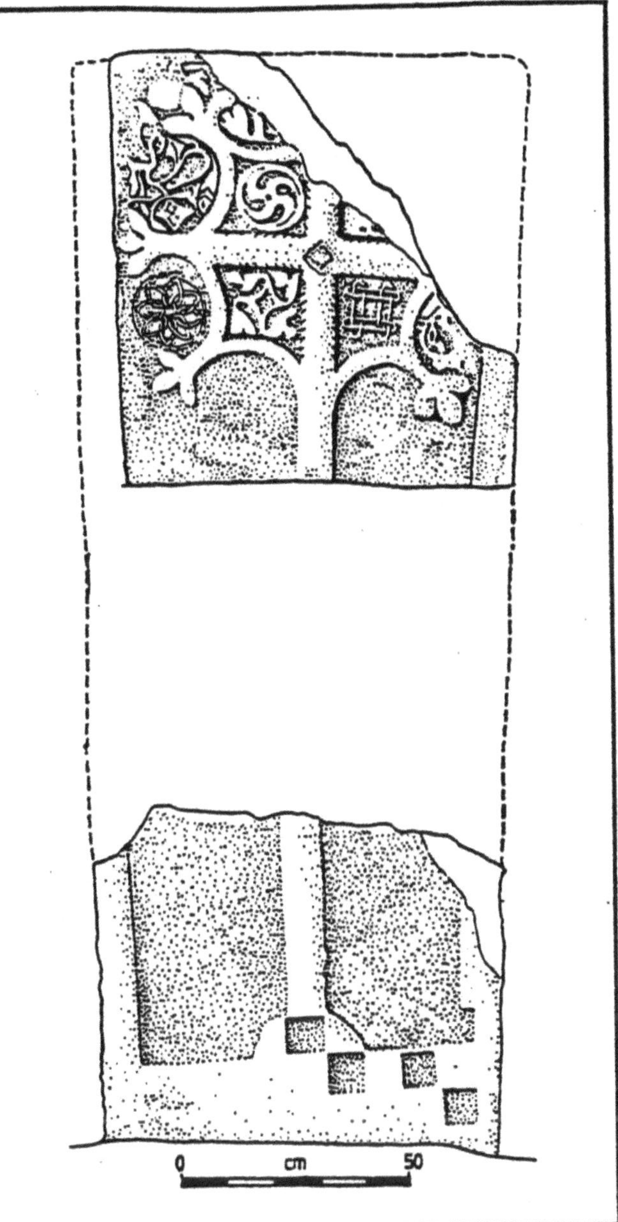

Fig. 11 Slab No. 1, Lisronagh (after Maher 1992).

It is possible, however, that future fieldwork in adjoining counties may result in the recognition of further groups to which some of these slabs may then be assigned.

Athassel Abbey: Each of these slabs - Athassel 1, 2, 8, 9 and 11 - bear different designs, but certain features may link them together. These include similarities in the style of the trefoil terminals, in the circular knops beneath the cross-heads and in the narrow form of the cross-stems. Perhaps these slabs were executed by the same carver or group of carvers.

Athassel 1 features a very ornate, eight-armed, cruciform motif and carries an inscription to *Frater Joh....*(Fig. 24). The arms of the cross are unusual in that they each feature a trefoil at the mid-point as well as at the terminal. A broken circle composed of four segments occurs at the centre of

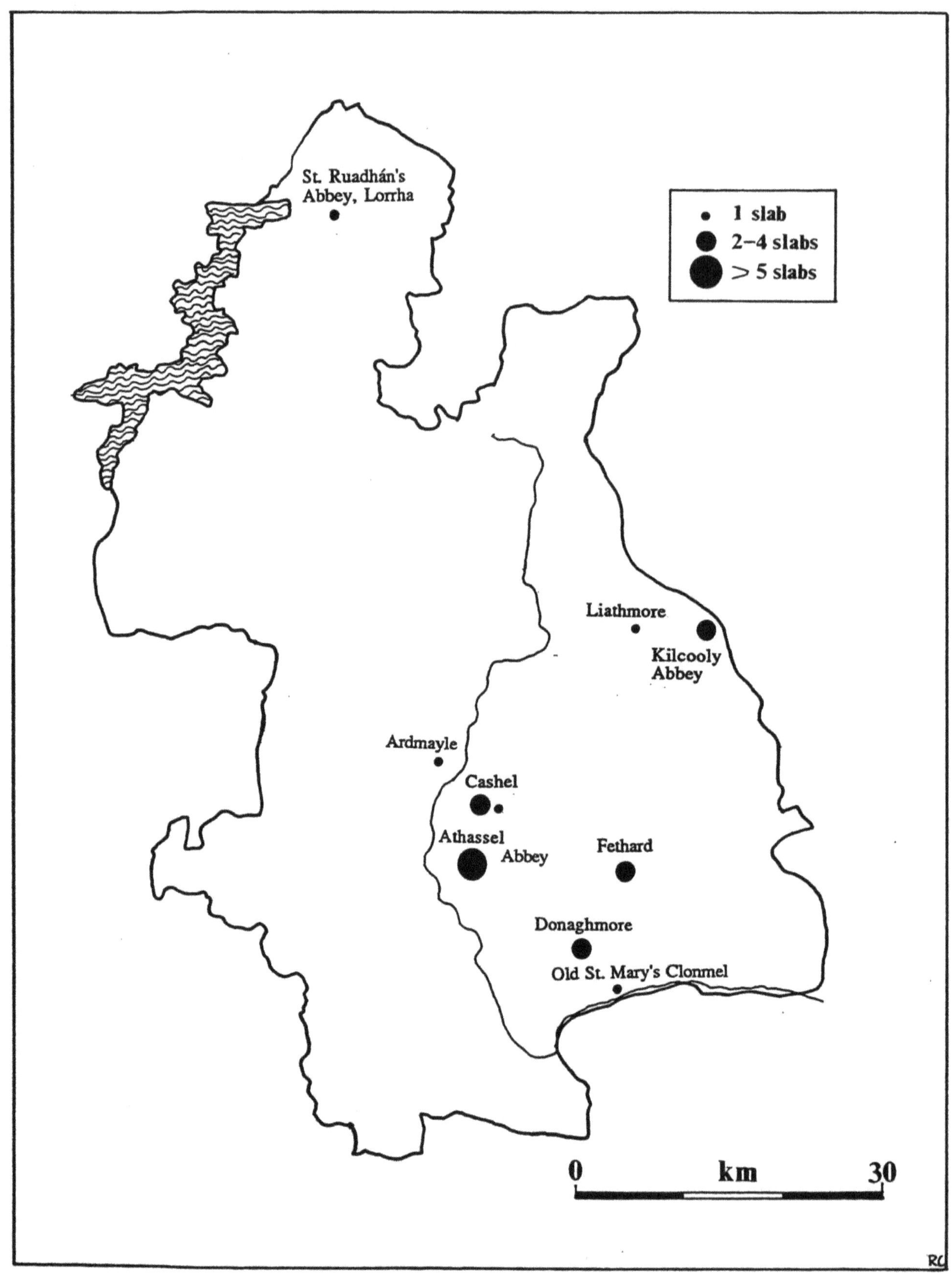

Fig. 12 Distribution of Group 5 grave-slabs in county Tipperary.

the cross and encloses a small diagonal cross. The diagonal arms of the overall design emanate from this lesser cross, whereas the vertical and horizontal arms commence within its angles. Three trefoils spring in a vegetal-like fashion from both sides of the base of the design. This finely executed design is unique in Tipperary, and has no known parallels outside of the county. A broadly similar design occurs on a slab in the centre of the choir of Tintern Abbey, Monmouth (Styan 1902, 33-34, pl. XXVI). The upper portion of this broken slab features an eight-armed cross in relief, and the arms terminate in trefoils similar to that of Athassel 1. Another close parallel between these slabs is the inner trefoils of the diagonal arms which are inwardly disposed. Styan dates the Tintern slab to the fourteenth century, and Athassel 1 may be broadly contemporary.

The design of Athassel 2 consists of an incised outline cross-head on a slender shaft, the base of which no longer survives. Each arm, with distinctly lobate trefoil terminals, emanates from the lozenge-shaped centre of the cross-head. A pair of lobed tendril-like features extend out from the dexter arm, however, only a single such feature extends from the dexter side of the vertical arms. While there are many parallels for the basic cross-head design, there is only one known parallel for the additional lobed tendril-like features: this occurs at the Dominican Abbey, Cashel, on slab no. 7. The other feature which these two slabs share is the knop, formed from an outline circle, which occurs beneath the cross-head from which the cross-stem emanates. Perhaps these slabs are the work of the same carver or school of carvers. The sites are only five miles apart, and parallels have already been drawn on architectural grounds between Athassel and Cashel friary by Leask (1960, 96). Contact between these two sites in a sculptural as well as an architectural context is likely.

Athassel 8 features an incised, outline, equal-armed cross with curved angles, enclosed by a circle which rests on the cross-shaft. The lower angles of the cross feature quatrefoils, while the upper angles feature curvilinear abstract motifs. The cross-stem emanates from a circular knop located at the base of the cross-head, and this terminates in a quatrefoil. This particular design is unique among the Tipperary collection and no parallels are known from outside of the county. However, parallels for the quatrefoiled motifs in the lower angles of the cross-head can be seen on a slab from St. John-sub-Castro Church, Lewes, Sussex (Styan 1902, 26, pl. X). In the latter case the cross-head is also enclosed by a circle, and the four angles of the cross feature these quatrefoiled motifs. Styan dates this slab to the fourteenth century.

The cross-head of Athassel 9 is also enclosed by an outline circle. In this case the cross-head takes the form of an interlaced eight-armed cross with trefoiled terminals. The centre of the cross-head is occupied by a simple floral motif, composed of eight triangular segments. While there is only one close parallel for this design in Tipperary, there are a number of related examples known from elsewhere in Ireland and Britain. These include two fourteenth-century slabs in St. Canice's Cathedral, Kilkenny (Bradley 1985, cat. no. 12, fig. 12; cat. no. 5, fig. 14). A slab from Gainford, dated by Ryder to the late thirteenth-early fourteenth century, features a similar design (Ryder 1985, no. 5, 85). Finally, in the porch of Raglan church, Monmouth, a fourteenth-century slab also features such a design (Styan 1902, 39, pl. XLVI). The only difference in the cross-head design between each of the above examples and Athassel 9 is that in the former cases the cross is not interlaced. The interlaced eight-armed cross-head was in use in Ireland up to the sixteenth century, and consequently the Athassel slab may be dated to anywhere between the fourteenth and the sixteenth centuries.

The Athassel 9 slab and that from Ardmayle are remarkably similar, the only difference being the design at the centre of the cross-head. In the case of Athassel 9 it consists of a floral motif formed of eight triangular segments, while the Ardmayle slab features a quatrefoiled motif. Athassel and Ardmayle are approximately eight miles apart, and perhaps these two slabs represent the work of a carver or school of carvers operating in this vicinity.

Athassel 11 also features an incised outline design. It consists of a cross surmounting a slender shaft which terminates in a knop and three trefoils. The centre of the cross-head features an eight-petalled rosette. Each arm is composed of a trefoil from which three stems emanate. The outer stems terminate in trefoils, while the central ones terminate in quinquefoils. Again there is no known parallel for this design in Tipperary or elsewhere in the country. There are a number of broadly similar parallels in England, however. An exact parallel for the base of Athassel 11 occurs on a fourteenth-century slab in Tintern Abbey, Monmouth (Styan 1902, 33-34, pl. XXVI). A broad, though not identical, parallel for the cross-head occurs on a contemporary slab from St. Mary Redcliffe, Bristol (*ibid*, 1902, 36, pl. XXXIII). Both slabs are richly foliated with multi-foiled arm terminals and an eight-petalled rosette motif occurs at the centre of the cross-head on each slab. A larger version of this rosette also occurs at the centre of the cross-head on a fourteenth-century slab in Aylesford, Kent (*ibid*, 1902, 36, pl. XXXV). Finally, another parallel for the three trefoil arm terminals occurs on a slab in Penshurst Church, Kent (*ibid*, 40, pl. LI). It should also be noted that the treatment of the trefoils is similar on both Athassel 11 and Kenshurst.

Overall it could be said of the Athassel slabs, though they each feature different designs, that a number of parallels can be drawn to indicate that the work may be that of the same carver or school of carvers. Such similarities include the forms of the trefoils at the arm terminals, the outline circles beneath the cross-heads, the narrow cross-stems, the use of the enclosing circle (in two cases) and the overall floriated impression of the slabs. Secondly, since most of the recognised parallels for these slabs are located in south and south-west England, perhaps these slabs represent the work of imported carvers from this part of England, or, alternatively, local carvers that spent some time in England and subsequently had contact with these sites.

St. Dominick's, Cashel: Four of the slabs at St. Dominick's Abbey (no's 1, 2, 7 and 9) feature different designs which have no known parallels elsewhere in the county. However, they do share certain features in common. While they cannot be grouped together because of the different crosses they feature, they may well have been the work of one carver or school.

St. Dominick's 1 consists of an incised outline cross. The cross-head, which is partly missing, appears to have consisted of an outline circle enclosing four smaller ones. The arrangement creates the effect of an equal-armed cross with expanded terminals. A small circle occurs beneath the cross-head, surmounting the cross-stem which terminates in a large trefoil. The only features that this slab has in common with St. Dominick's 2 and 9 are the small circle beneath the cross-head and the very large trefoiled base. Otherwise there are no known parallels for this slab in the county. However, it does appear to be related to the thirteenth-century four-circle cross in Britain (Ryder 1985, 16, fig. 5). In the case of St. Dominick's 2, the four circles seem to compose a cross-paté, which was common in the first three quarters of the twelfth century in Britain (*ibid*, 1985, 9). Broad parallels can yet again be drawn with slabs among Styan's collection. One relevant example occurs at the Chapter House, Westminster, and features four circles which compose the cross - "a distinctive feature of the thirteenth century" (Styan 1902, 21, pl. 1). Another broadly similar parallel occurs on a slab at St. Nicholas' Chapel in Canterbury Cathedral. In this case four penannular circles compose a cross-paté; Styan dates it to the thirteenth century (*ibid*, 1902, 42, pl. LVIII). Obviously the use of the four circles to form the cross was related to the 'bracelet'-cross (or the use of four penannular circles). Therefore, the closest links for St. Dominick's 1 in Tipperary is with the cross-design of Group 2 slabs, for which a thirteenth-fourteenth century date has been proposed.

St. Dominick's 2 consists of an incised outline cross. Each arm terminates in an extremely large trefoil. A small knop formed by an outline circle occurs beneath the cross-head, surmounting the cross-stem which terminates in another very large trefoil. On the sinister side of the cross-stem two rows of oblique lines occur forming a herringbone pattern. Portion of a similar design survives on the dexter side. The small circle beneath the cross-head and the terminating large trefoil are similar to those of St. Dominick's 9 and 1. The idea of enclosing the cross-head within an outline circle was also employed in St. Dominick's 1 and Athassel 8 and 9. The basic design of the cross-head is not unusual among Irish medieval grave-slabs, though the addition of the herringbone pattern is quite unique.

St. Dominick's 7 is a very unusual slab featuring an incised outline cross-stem, extending the length of the slab, terminating at each end in a fleur-de-lis. It also features a Lombardic inscription which, unfortunately, is illegible. No parallels or close affinities occur for this slab in Tipperary or elsewhere. Perhaps the design is unfinished or was meant to represent a crozier or some other ecclesiastical emblem.

The final slab at St. Dominick's Abbey, no. 9 (Fig. 43), is located in a recumbent position beneath the base of a pillar and its upper portion is missing. Parallels have already been drawn for the single-lobed features of this slab with Athassel 2. Again, the large trefoil base and the small outline circle beneath the cross-head is quite typical of the designs of the Dominican friary slabs in general.

Overall, even though the designs of each of the above four slabs are different, the style of the carving is quite similar, and, as at Athassel, the slabs are probably the work of one carver or of one particular school. Based on parallels with English slabs and on certain features, such as the outlining quatrefoil design of St. Dominick's 2, a thirteenth-fourteenth century date is suggested here.

Augustinian Abbey, Fethard: Two slabs occur at this site- no's 4 and 5 - which feature simple crosses with large trefoiled terminals emanating from a lozenge-shaped centre. Both are possibly of sixteenth- or early seventeenth-century date.

Fethard Abbey 4 features a cross carved in relief, with the transverse terminals ending in trefoils and with the upper one merging with the top of the slab. Three cross-bands occur at the base of the cross-head. A similar feature occurs at the base of the cross-shaft, surmounting a pillar-base form. A sun motif occupies the upper dexter corner of the slab, while a moon motif occupies the upper sinister one. The slab features no inscription or date. It appears to have acted as a tomb lid, as is indicated by the presence of the roll moulding on the sinister side. There are only two broadly similar slabs in the county - Fethard Abbey 5 and a seventeenth-century slab in the nearby Holy Trinity Church (Long 1907, 178). The main difference between the latter two slabs and Fethard Abbey 4 is that the arms of the cross on the former examples do not merge with the outer border. However, the base of the design of Fethard Abbey 4 and 5 is quite similar. This cross-head design was a typical thirteenth-fourteenth century form in both Ireland and Britain.

Fethard Abbey 5 may also have functioned as a tomb lid, as it also features a roll moulding on its sinister side and across its top. Again, the cross is carved in relief and each arm, emanating from a lozenge-shaped centre, terminates in a large trefoil. A narrow border occurs along the edge of the cross design. Three cross-bands occur at the base of the cross-head and at the base of the cross-shaft, where they surmount a possible pillar-base form. The slab also bears an inscription in Roman lettering which, unfortunately, bears no date. The only parallels for this slab in the county are Fethard Abbey 4 and the dated slab in the Holy Trinity Church.

Based on the Roman lettering of Fethard Abbey 5, the overall size and style of slabs 4 and 5 and their close similarities to the slab at Holy Trinity Church, which dates to 1635, it is suggested that both no's 4 and 5 are late sixteenth-early seventeenth century in date. Because there are only three such slabs in Tipperary, perhaps they represent the work of a single carver. Since the cross-head design of these two slabs is of typical thirteenth-fourteenth century date, it should be obvious that any proposed stylistic development of grave-slabs will not be without its exceptions.

Donaghmore: The two slabs from this site have been assigned to the miscellaneous category. Donaghmore 1 (Fig. 26) is a limestone slab surviving in three portions and is located inside the Romanesque church. The design, which is in relief, consists of a cross with each arm terminating in simple trefoils. Two cross-bands occur at the base of the cross-head and one is located at the base of the cross-shaft, surmounting a pillar-base form. This is the only grave-slab of its kind in the county. However, there are many such cross-head designs occurring elsewhere with variations in the fleur-de-lis. These include, for example, a fifteenth or sixteenth century slab in Westham Church, Sussex (Styan 1902, 25, pl. VII) and a broadly similar example at St. Paul's Church, Jarrow. In the latter case the design is incised and consists of a straight-armed cross with cusped and fleur-de-lis terminals. It is dated to the late fourteenth or early fifteenth century (Ryder 1985, 100, no. 1). In Ireland the closest parallel occurs in Clonfert Cathedral, Co. Galway (Atkinson 1906, 559). This rectangular slab dates to 1612 and features a straight-armed cross with each arm terminating in a fleur-de-lis. The straight-armed cross with fleur-de-lis terminals was more popular in the seventeenth century, and was often featured on slabs decorated with the symbols of the passion. It is quite common for the crown of thorns to be suspended from such cross-heads, as is seen, for example, on the seventeenth-century slab in St. Mary's, New Ross, Co. Wexford (Vigors 1903, 490).

Based on the dates of the parallels given above, Donaghmore 1 could date to anywhere between the fourteenth and seventeenth centuries. Taking into account the cross-base, the slight taper and its overall simplicity, however, a late fourteenth to fifteenth century date is likely.

Unlike the previous slab, Donaghmore 2 (Fig. 27) is of sandstone and features a design unique in this corpus. The cross-head, which is in relief, consists of an equal-armed cross with bifid terminals and a lozenge-shaped centre set in a sunken circle. A broad outlined shaft occurs beneath the cross-head, on either side of which a broad, rectilinear panel with bifid tops occurs. The slab is undated. Setting the cross-head within a sunken circle is relatively uncommon in Ireland, though it was a feature of some early medieval slabs. However, there are quite a number of examples of the sunken cross-head style in Ryder's Durham collection (1985). The cross-head, in fact, calls to mind Ryder's 'bracelet-cross' (1985, 9-10) - a cross formed of four penannular circles. Donaghmore 2 may be an example of this cross-form at its most basic and consequently may date to the thirteenth or fourteenth century.

Liathmore: Liathmore 1, which consists of a badly broken sandstone slab, is also unique in this corpus (Fig. 39). In fact no known parallels occur for it in Ireland or Britain. The design, which is in relief, occurs at the top of the slab and consists of a badly worn human figure with a long robe and with outstretched arms. The position of the arms along with the type of clothing call to mind the Triumphant rather than the Crucified Christ. This sort of iconography is unknown among Medieval grave-slabs elsewhere. It is quite possible that this is an early slab, perhaps twelfth century in date, on the basis of the parallels between the dress of Christ here and on some twelfth century high crosses (Henry 1970, 127-8).

Old St. Mary's, Clonmel: Old St. Mary's 1 is a sixteenth-century slab and is the only one of its kind in the county (Fig. 41). It features a ringed cross carved in relief, the arms of which have bifid terminals, surmounting a more elaborate diagonal cross. This cross-head design surmounts a unique cross-shaft which is fluted and tapers towards the top. The cross terminates in an elaborate pillar-base form. Overall, the design of this slab, which is dated 1583, is quite impressive. Unfortunately no parallels or even broadly similar examples are known.

Kilcooley: Three out of the six slabs at Kilcooley Abbey feature seven-armed crosses - no's 1, 2 and 5 - and these are dealt with in Chapter Four; the others - no's 3, 4 and 6 - feature miscellaneous designs. Kilcooley 3 is of significance for two main reasons: firstly, it is one of the only two slabs in this corpus to feature a selection of the symbols of the passion; secondly, it is the only grave-slab, with the exception of Liathmore 1, to feature a human figure (Fig. 35). The cross which it features consists of a straight-armed Latin example from which the crown of thorns is suspended. The passion symbols are distributed around the cross. The figure of an abbot, which is carved in false relief below the cross, is of the general form of the period. Even though the plain Latin example, the passion symbols and the carved figure are not uncommon among Irish sepulchral monuments, this slab still remains unique in this corpus. Perhaps this is so because the slab is that of an ecclesiastic and that the main design is not the cross, the passion symbols or the carved figure, but all three together. The slab dates to 1463 and commemorates Philip O'Molwanayn.

Kilcooley 4 is a limestone slab which features no inscription or date (Fig. 36). Not only is the design of this slab unique in this corpus, but also its shape. The design, which is carved in relief, occurs on the top portion of the slab in a sunken rectangular panel. It features an eight-armed cross formed of penannular circles around an eight-spoked centre. The only close parallel for this slab is in Whickham (Ryder 1985, 118, no. 2), and features part of a Lombardic inscription. Ryder suggests a mid-thirteenth century date for it. The angled-base which Kilcooley 4 features is quite rare. In the Dominican church in Athenry, county Galway, however, a seventeenth century rectangular slab features a similar base (Macalister 1913, 210, no. 1). This base is not necessarily indicative of a late date, however, and an earlier date might be appropriate for the Kilcooley slab. Taking into consideration the distinct taper of the slab, its wide chamfer, its likeness to the Whickham slab and the use of the 'bracelet-cross' or penannular circles, a thirteenth to fourteenth century date is suggested here.

The third slab at Kilcooley is no. 6 (Fig. 37) - a mid-fifteenth century slab. The main theme of the design is centred on the symbols of the passion - a selection of which are carved on the upper portion of the slab. There is no actual cross-head as such, rather the diagonally disposed lance and sponge take its place. A shaft featuring vegetal-like motifs extends from just below the passion symbols and terminates in a stepped base. This is the only slab, along with Kilcooley 3, that features a selection of the these passion symbols in this corpus.

St. Patrick's Cathedral, Cashel: St. Patrick's Cathedral 5 features a design in relief, which is otherwise not represented in this corpus (Fig. 46). It consists of a cross with each arm terminating in elaborate and florid multi-foiled terminals. The arms emanate from a lozenge-shaped centre. A motif formed of three cross-bands occurs at the base of the cross-head, surmounting the cross-shaft which terminates in a pillar form. The slab bears the date 1524. Though the pillar-base form of the cross is quite common during the sixteenth century, the cross-head of slab no. 5 is not. It is a variation, however, of the popular cross with simple trefoil terminals emanating from a lozenge-shaped centre. The treatment of these arm terminals is unique among the Tipperary grave-slabs.

GROUP 6: FRAGMENTARY SLABS

The six slabs which form this small group are each very poorly preserved. Consequently it is not possible to assign them with any certainty to the above groupings. Nevertheless, each exhibit characteristics which clearly indicate that they are of medieval date.

St. Ruadhan's, Lorrha: St. Ruadhan's 1 is a tapered slab which survives in two portions. Its decorated surface is rather worn and the design is difficult to decipher. All that survives is a broad outline cross-shaft surmounted by what appears to be the lower arm of a cross-head. Based on this surviving arm the cross appears to have been of equal-armed type with expanded terminals, similar in form to the diagonal cross on Old St. Mary's 1. Unfortunately the upper portion of the slab is missing.

St. Dominick's Friary, Cashel: Dominican Friary 3 survives in a very worn state. All that survives of the design is an incised outline cross-stem. The cross-head does not survive. An early modern inscription is incised onto the upper portion of the slab. A new surface appears to have been prepared for this inscription, thus eliminating the cross-head.

St. Patrick's, Cathedral, Cashel: Four unclassifiable slabs occur at St. Patrick's Cathedral, Cashel - no's 8, 12, 22 and 24. Only the lower portions of incised outline cross-stems survive on no's 8 and 12. The remainder of the decorated surfaces of these slabs are very badly worn and chipped. In relation to the majority of the other slabs at this site, which are of sixteenth century date, these appear to be earlier, perhaps fourteenth century.

The upper portion of the decorated surface of St. Patrick's 22 is rather worn and only the lower section of the design survives. The surviving design, which is incised, consists of two broad panels with pointed ends. These extend two-thirds of the way up the slab (and are paralleled in a general way on a number of slabs which form the sixteenth century Group 4 slabs).

Cashel 24 consists of a portion of a slab with a chamfered sinister edge. As with no's 8, 12 and 22, the decorated surface is very worn. The design, which is incised, consists of the lower segment of an outline circle surmounting a circular knop, from which the outline cross-shaft emanates, terminating in a stepped base.

Overall, based on the meagre survival of the above designs, speculation about their original form is difficult.

GROUP 7: PLAIN SLABS

There are only fifteen grave-slabs in the county which do not feature any design. These slabs occur at Athassel Augustinian abbey (x6), Liathmore (x1), Dominican Friary, Cashel (x4), Holycross Abbey (x3), and Knockgraffon Church (x1). In all cases, except for Knockgraffon, these occur alongside other medieval grave-slabs which do bear designs. The first six slabs occur at Athassel abbey - Athassel 4, 6, 10, 12, 13 and 14. Athassel 6 is the only slab in this group to feature an inscription:

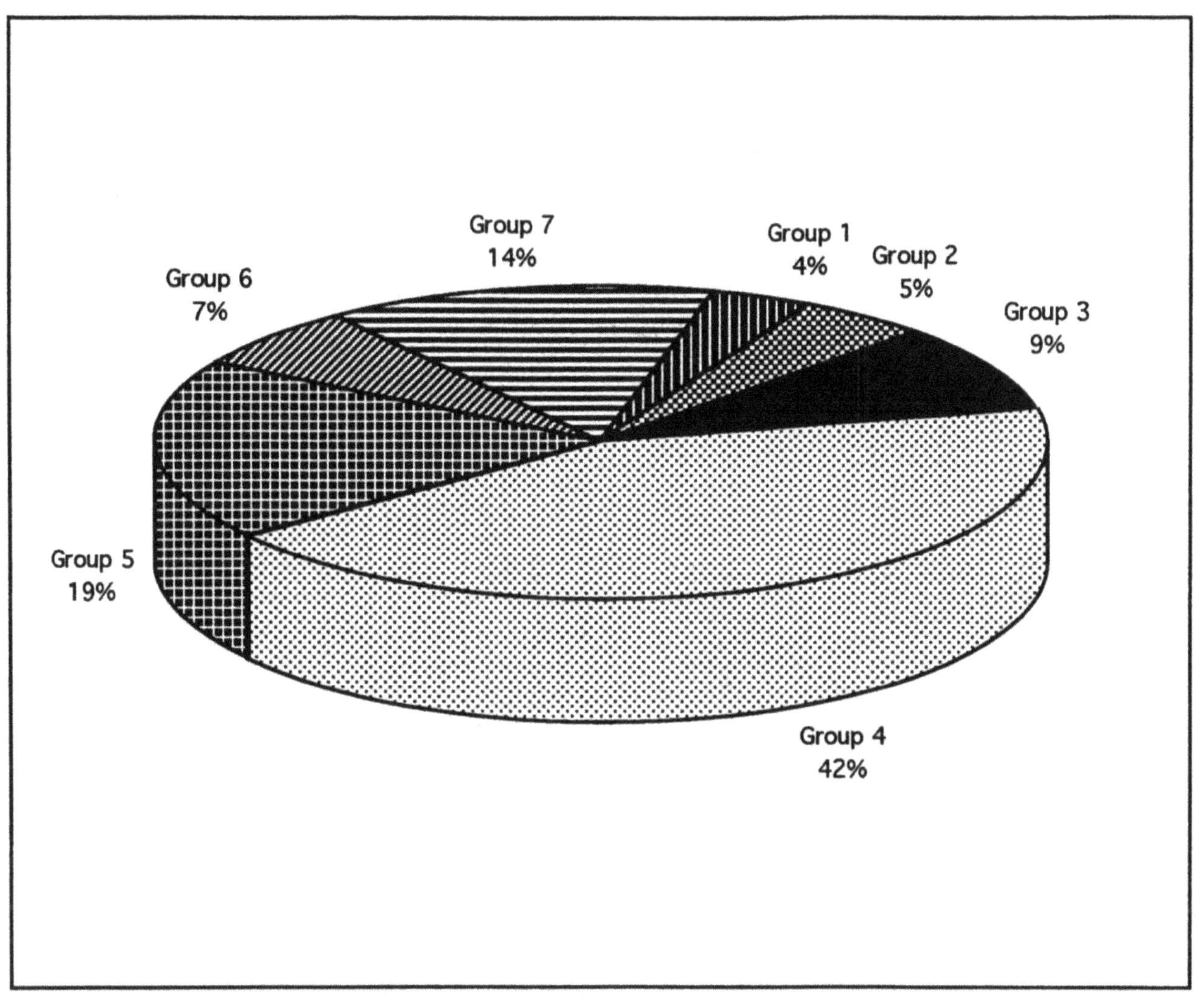

Fig. 13 Pie-chart indicating the frequency of occurrence of the various groups of medieval grave-slabs from county Tipperary.

this occurs in Lombardic lettering and reads *HIC IACET FRATER THOMAS*. All of the six slabs, except for Athassel 10, survive only as portions or fragments. However, they all seem to be tapered and to feature chamfered edges.

Liathmore 2 consists of a sandstone slab of rectangular shape. Unfortunately, little of the original edge along both sides of the slab survives. No inscription occurs and the upper surface of the slab is badly worn. There is no doubt, however, that this is a medieval grave-slab, due to its likeness in shape to Liathmore 1 and the similar type of stone used in both cases.

Four of the nine grave-slabs that occur at St. Dominick's Abbey, Cashel, do not feature any evidence for designs. These comprise St. Dominick's 4, 5, 6 and 8. The latter two slabs are complete, whereas no's 4 and 5 are only portions of slabs. In each of the four cases the slabs (or portions of slabs) are tapered and no inscription occurs on any of them.

Holycross 2, 3 and 4 consist of portions of tapered slabs with no designs or inscriptions. Finally, Knockgraffon 1 - a sixteenth century slab which commemorates the Rector of Knockgraffon - has no traces of a design but does bear a fragmentary inscription. Again only portion of the slab survives and its original edges are chamfered.

Overall only two of the fifteen plain slabs bear an inscription - Athassel 6 (Lombardic) and Knockgraffon 1 (Black Letter). There are three possible reasons as to why these slabs do not apparently feature any designs. Firstly, perhaps they were originally decorated but this no longer survives due to their worn nature. However, one would expect some part of the design to survive. (Rubbings were taken of a selection of these slabs in order to determine whether traces of any designs survived, but the results of this exercise were negative). On the other hand, perhaps these slabs were never meant to have designs, or perhaps they were making a social statement and were used by the lower classes. Finally, it is also possible that these were unfinished slabs, or even, roughouts, that were prepared in advance of commissions. Such grave-slabs are not uncommon and are distributed throughout the country on the same sites as decorated examples.

CHAPTER FOUR

MOTIFS, EMBLEMS AND SYMBOLS

One of the more interesting aspects of medieval grave-slabs is their iconography. Only a minority of the slabs in this corpus have no evidence for design, with ninety out of the total of one-hundred and seven featuring some sort of ornamentation ranging from simple incised crosses to more elaborate and complicated types. The primary emblem is the cross, which is represented in many forms. Secondary symbols also occur, but on only a relatively minor cross-section of the Tipperary group. These include passion symbols, floral patterns, ecclesiastical symbols, heraldic emblems and some Celtic motifs. The study of these is of great importance and occasionally gives an insight into the occupation, rank and sex of the people commemorated, and into local medieval mortuary practices. The representation of secondary symbols on grave-slabs throughout Ireland and Britain was not as consistent as the representation of the cross and grave-slab forms. In Ryder's study on the Durham cross-slabs, for example, a good proportion of the slabs feature secondary emblems, especially the sword, shears and chalice (1985, 18-29). In Ireland, however, such symbols were not common. On the other hand, however, the symbols of the passion feature far more frequently on the Irish slabs than on the English examples.

In this corpus only two slabs feature the passion symbols - Kilcooley 3 and 6. Other symbols and motifs are represented only once in most cases: Celtic motifs - Lisronagh 1; ecclesiastical emblems - Kilcooley 3; skull and cross-bones - Old St. Mary's 2, and the *sol et lunulae* - Fethard Abbey 4. Heraldic shields, on the other hand, occur on Fethard Abbey 2, 3, 11, Old St. Mary's 1 and St. Patrick's Cathedral 15.

THE CROSS

As mentioned above, the cross is the primary emblem found on medieval grave-slabs and occurs in many forms (Fig. 14). This calls to mind the early decree by Kenneth, King of Scotland, that one should "esteem every sepulchre or gravestone sacred, and adorn it with the sign of the cross, which take care you do not so much as tread on" (Gough 1786, 35). Stylistically the design of the cross changed throughout the medieval period, but whether there is a corresponding change in its symbolic significance is another question. The different cross-forms may represent a number of things, but their fundamental connotation is the blood sacrifice of Christ for man, leading to resurrection and salvation. Their occurrence on a grave-slab, therefore, represents the aspiring salvation of the individual Christian buried beneath it.

Another term often used in reference to the cross is the Tree of Life, especially in relation to foliated/floriated cross-forms. Included in this category are the simple trefoil and fleur-de-lis forms. The fleur-de-lis is the royal insignia of France. Clovis, King of the Franks, chose it as the emblem of purification by baptism when he embraced Christianity - the lily symbolising purity. It is frequently used in funerary art. There are divergent theories, however, as to its origin. For example, botanists see it as an arbitrary form of the iris - used as a primitive sceptre by early chieftains. There are two main opposing schools of thought, therefore, comprising those that see it as a symbol of purity and those who regard it as a war symbol. Evidence may be found to support both theories (Cadogan Rothery 1994, 166).

The use of foliated/floriated cross-forms to represent the Tree of Life has different symbolic connotations. Examples of slabs featuring such cross-forms include Athassel 1 and 11 (Fig. 24) and Kilcooley 6 (Fig. 37). The Tree "represents ordered growth and links earth and heaven rooted in darkness, its crown expands into light" (Cook 1974, 6). This mysterious and powerful image has been used in primitive mythology right up to the twentieth century. As well as the tree symbolically linking heaven and earth, it also represents the beginning and end of time - the Alpha and Omega, the former being the Tree at the centre of the Garden of Eden, the latter the tree at the centre of Jerusalem. The link between the Cross of Christ and the Tree of Life has been recognised since Judaeo-Christian times.

The other obvious feature of significance of the cross-form found on medieval slabs is the stepped base, representing the free-standing cross which signifies the Crucifixion. Examples of this type include Marlfield 1 and Kilcooley 6. The stepped base is not a very common feature in this corpus, with only nine examples represented out of a total of one hundred and seven. Thus, while the cross is the primary emblem, it is represented in a number of ways and carries numerous religious connotations.

Before leaving this discussion on the cross it is worth mentioning an interesting metalwork parallel to the type most commonly found on Irish medieval grave-slabs. This is the beautifully decorated Ballylongford processional cross of the fifteenth century. From county Kerry, this is made of brass, solder and gilt and bears a Latin inscription. The points of parallel occur in the arm terminals which are floriated, in the knop which occurs beneath the crucified Christ and in the Black Letter inscription. It is of importance to note that

Fig. 14 A representative sample of cross-head types from medieval grave-slabs in county Tipperary.

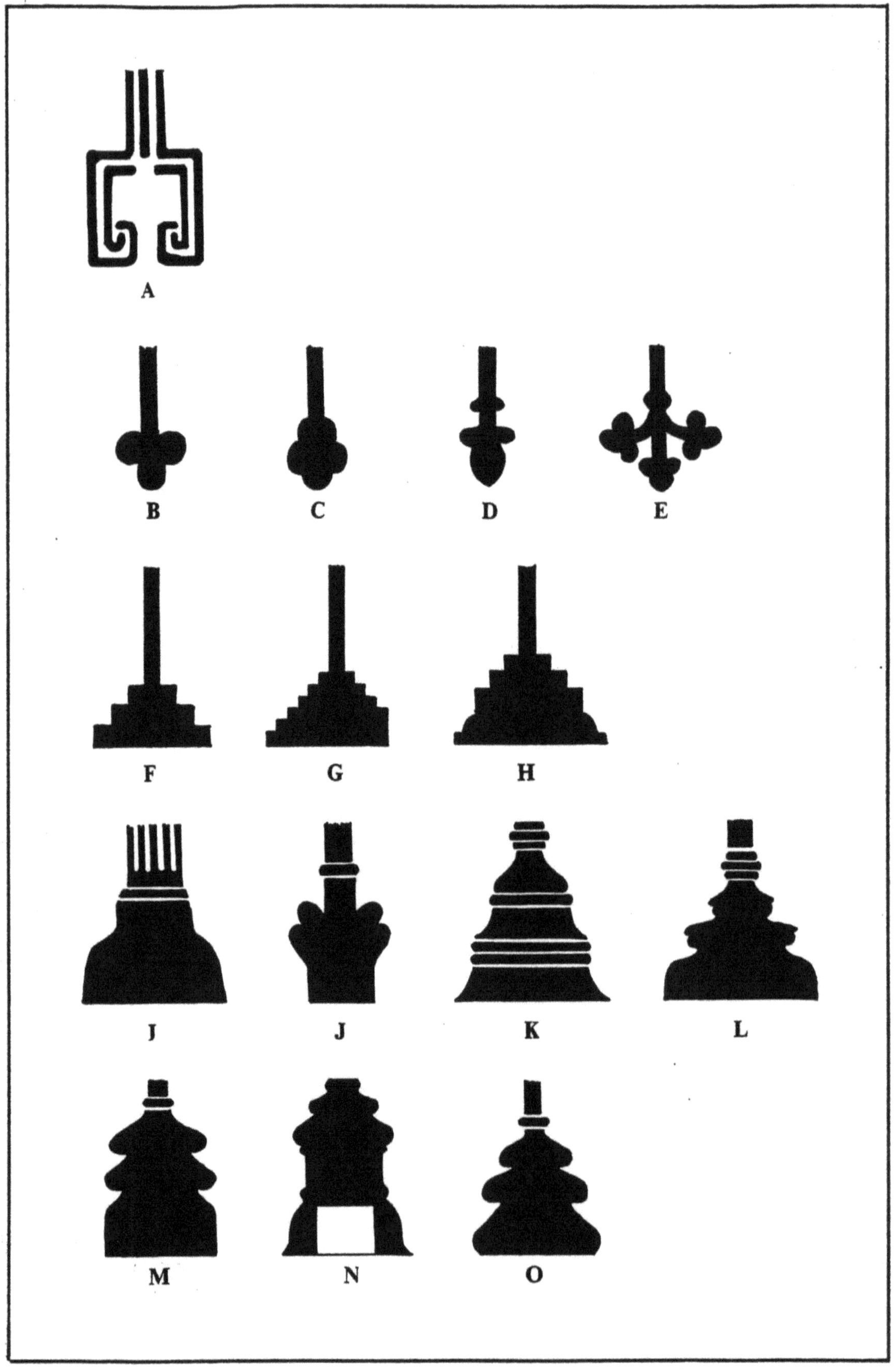

Fig. 15 A representative sample of cross-base types from medieval grave-slabs in county Tipperary.

such features, which are so common among the cross-inscribed grave-slabs, were not confined to stone carving only and were also employed by the metal-worker. The Ballylongford cross is a typical example of a late processional Gothic cross.

Cross-heads

The different forms of cross-heads selected for identifying the main groups of grave-slabs in Tipperary have already been dealt with in detail in Chapter Three. The following list, however, is a summary which serves to identify the frequency, distribution and dating of the main cross-head forms occurring in the county.

THE RINGED CROSS (Fig. 14 a): There is only one example of this type in Tipperary: Coolmundry 1. It consists of a sub-circular cross-head of ringed form with three short arms. There are strong early medieval influences evident here, thus placing it amongst the earliest of the recorded cross-forms.

THE 'BRACELET' CROSS (Fig.14 b-e): This type is represented by five examples: Two-Mile-Borris 1, Donaghmore 2, Kilcooley Abbey 4, Derrynaflan 1 and St. Patrick's Cathedral 1. In the cases of Two-Mile-Borris, Derrynaflan and St. Patrick's Cathedral the cross-head is composed of four penannular circles. The Kilcooley example is made up of eight such circles. Three of the above examples - Two-Mile-Borris, Derrynaflan and St. Patrick's Cathedral - also belong to the head-slab tradition. This factor, along with the broadly similar parallels in England, put this cross-form in the thirteenth to fourteenth century date bracket.

THE SIMPLE FLORIATED CROSS (Fig. 14 f-l): Seven examples can be assigned to this group: Athassel Abbey 2, Donaghmore 1, Augustinian Abbey, Fethard 4 and 5, Holycross Abbey 10, Marlfield 1 and St. Dominick's, Cashel 2. Three of the above have a lozenge-shaped centre, three are plain and one is segmented. Variations also occur to the number of arms: four have three arms and the remainder are four-armed. The predominant feature is the simple large trefoil at each arm terminal. The dating of this particular type is not straightforward. All of the above examples, except for Augustinian Abbey, Fethard 4 and 5, can be assigned to the thirteenth and fourteenth centuries on the basis of their overall form. The other two, however, appear to be sixteenth or seventeenth century in date. See Chapter Three for more detail.

THE RICHLY FOLIATED CROSS (Fig. 14 m-p): Four examples fall into this category: Athassel Abbey 1, 8, 9 and 11. The style of the cross-head in each case, though not exactly the same, is broadly similar in its style of execution. This is based on the attention to detail and the treatment of its arm terminals. It appears that these slabs are the work of one carver, and that they are peculiar to this site. It is difficult to assign a date to this cross-head type. Based on English parallels, however, and the presence of a Lombardic inscription on one of them, along with the obvious taper of the slabs, a fourteenth century date is indicated.

THE SEVEN-ARMED SEGMENTED CROSS-HEAD (Fig. 14 q-s): There are thirty-six examples of this type in the county. Two occur at Old St. Mary's, Clonmel (no's 2 and 3) eleven at the Augustinian Abbey, Fethard (no's 1, 2, 6 and 7 - 14) six at Holy Cross (no's 1, 6, 7, 8, 9, and 11), one at Marlfield (no. 2), three at Kilcooley (no's 1, 2 and 5), one at St. John's, Cashel (no. 1), sixteen at St. Patrick's Cathedral, Cashel (no's 2, 3, 4, 6, 9, 11, 13, 14 - 19, 21, 23 and 25) and one at Holy Trinity Church, Fethard (no.1). The basic design is similar in all cases, though variation does occur in the treatment of the fleur-de-lis motif. Dating of this group is straightforward as a good proportion of the slabs featuring this cross-head type carry sixteenth and early seventeenth century dates.

Cross-bases

BOXED TERMINATION (Fig. 15 a): Baptist Grange 1 and Kiltinan 1 and 2 all feature variations of this type. It consists of either a plain rectangle-like pedestal or else one that terminates in volutes (for example, Kiltinan 2). As has already been discussed in Chapter Three, this type of base has parallels in early medieval contexts. On that basis, and along with the overall form of these slabs, a twelfth to thirteenth century date is suggested here.

SIMPLE TREFOIL BASE (Fig. 15 b-e): There are eleven examples of this type: Athassel Abbey 3, 5, 7, 8 and 11, Holy Trinity church, Fethard 2, Holy Cross 5 and St. Dominick's 4. This cross-base type, which consists of a single, simple trefoil and slight variations thereof, can be dated to the thirteenth and fourteenth centuries on the basis of parallels elsewhere (for example, St. Canice's Cathedral, Kilkenny) and on their overall form.

THE STEPPED BASE (Fig.15 f-h): Nine grave-slabs feature stepped bases in the county. These occur on Holy Cross 6, Marlfield 1 and 2, Kilcooley Abbey 6 and St. Patrick's Cathedral, Cashel 1, 14, 18, 20 and 24. Three of these examples - St. Patrick's 14, 18 and 20 - feature sixteenth-century dates. The presence of the stepped base on St. Patrick's 1, however, which is a head-slab, and for which a thirteenth to fourteenth century date has been indicated, suggest the recurrent use of this type of cross-base throughout the Medieval period.

PILLAR-BASE FORM (Fig.15 i-o): This is the most popular of all the base types with thirty-two examples occurring in the county. These include Old St. Mary's 1 and 2, Donaghmore 1, Fethard Augustinian Abbey 1, 3, 4, 5, 7, 8, 9, 10 and 11, Fethard Holy Trinity 1, Holy Cross 1, 7, 8, 9, and Kilcooley 1 and 2, and St. John's Cathedral, Cashel 2, 3, 4, 5, 6, 7, 13, 15, 16, 21, 23 and 25. This base-type can be dated to the fifteenth, sixteenth and seventeenth centuries, based on dated examples and overall form.

Fig. 16 A selection of common passion symbols.

PASSION SYMBOLS

The earliest surviving depiction of the passion symbols in Ireland occurs on the Domhnach Airgid shrine, made *c.* 1340-50 (Roe 1983, 530). The *arma christi* are also commonly depicted on heraldic shields, altars, tombs and tomb niches throughout Ireland. The occurrence of passion symbols not only provides information regarding personal devotion, but also, as is noted in Chapter Seven, an insight into the political history of the later medieval period.

There is evidence for the *arma christi* occurring on grave-slabs dating from the fifteenth to the seventeenth centuries. In the context of this catalogue, only two examples - Kilcooley 3 and 6 - both of which are fifteenth century in date, feature a good selection of these symbols. Only one slab features the skull and cross-bones, and only two feature the *sol et lunulae* motif - Old St. Mary's 2 and Fethard Abbey 4. However, there are quite a number of seventeenth century slabs in Tipperary which feature a broad selection of these symbols, with examples occurring in Holycross Abbey, Loughmore, Fethard and Lorrha.

Outside of county Tipperary sixteenth century examples of passion symbols occur at St. Canice's Cathedral, Kilkenny (Bradley 1985, cat. no. 50, fig. 36, cat. no. 57, fig. 40 and cat. no. 63, fig. 44), Rathmore, Co. Meath (Fitzgerald 1908, 435), the 'French Church', Co. Waterford (Garstin 1907, 190), Killeen church, Co. Meath (Fitzgerald 1911, 416) and Kilmacow, Co. Kilkenny (Manning 1902, 228). Seventeenth century examples occur at Tullow churchyard, Co. Carlow (Fitzgerald 1913-14, 19), St. Mary's New Ross, Co. Wexford (Vigors 1903, 491) and at St. Multose Church, Kinsale (Darling 1895, 46). There is no obvious difference in the manner of depiction of these symbols. The cross-form along with which they feature, however, varies. The seven-armed fleur-de-lis cross was one form, while the plain Latin cross was another. It was a common feature to have the Crown of Thorns suspended from the cross-head, and examples of this occur at Kinsale (Darling 1895, 46), Wexford (Vigors 1903, 491) and Rathmore, Co. Meath (Fitzgerald 1908, 435).

There are almost fifty different symbols in the *arma christi* repertoire. However, only a limited selection of these is represented at any one time. The following are the symbols most often illustrated: the hammer, ladder, cock and pot, *sol et lunulae*, skull and cross-bones, sponge and lance, dice, nails, scourges, scourging pillar, one-piece garment and the Crown of Thorns (Fig. 16). Where such a symbol occurs on its own it is usually either the *sol et lunulae* motif - for example Fethard Abbey 4 and the Hurley slab in the 'French Church' ruins, Waterford (Garstin 1907, 190) - or the skull and cross-bones - for example Old St. Mary's 2. A feature worthy of note on the latter slab is the epigram *Memento Mori*, which is inscribed across the base of the slab. Translated it means 'Remember Death' - a rather strong choice of words, obviously indicating the significant influence of death in the Medieval period. This point is discussed further in Chapter Seven.

Kilcooley 3 and 6, both dating to the fifteenth century, are the only two examples of pre-seventeenth century grave-slabs featuring the symbols of the passion known in Tipperary. Kilcooley 3 (Fig. 35) is quite an interesting and large slab bearing the *arma christi* - a plain Latin cross divides the shield into four unequal quadrants. The Crown of Thorns is suspended from the cross-beam, which is pierced by two nails. The ladder occurs on the sinister side of the cross and the lance and sponge on the dexter side. The sponge is encircled by intertwined ropes and it also serves the purpose of the scourging post. Below these are the one-piece garment, two scourges, three dice and a hammer. On the sinister side, below the hammer, are the pincers and the cock and pot. Occupying the lower half of the slab is the figure of an abbot in vestments. Kilcooley 6 is not so elaborate, though the passion symbols again occupy the upper portion of the slab, surmounting the cross-shaft which features foliated forms - probably intended to represent the Tree of Life. The shaft terminates in a stepped, calvary-like base. The cup and lance, from which the Crown of Thorns is suspended, act as the cross-head. The ladder occurs on its dexter side and the hammer on the sinister side. Below these are the pincers, one-piece garment and a scourge. Overall this slab carries three main features of religious significance: the symbols of the passion, the Tree of Life image and the stepped base. Again, these are not mere designs, but strong Christian symbols.

The following is a list of the main Passion symbols that occur in the Tipperary group:

IHS MONOGRAM: The first three letters of the Greek word for Jesus - *IHSOUS*. These letters are written as three separate initials - *Iesus Homien Salvator* - Jesus the Saviour of mankind.
COCK: This is used to symbolise the sin of Peter.
CROSS: The symbol of Christ's sacrifice.
CROWN OF THORNS: The symbol of Christ's suffering.
DICE: Representing the casting of lots for Christ's clothes.
HAMMER: Used in nailing Christ to the cross
LANCE: Used to pierce Christ's side.
MOON: This symbol occurs frequently in Christian art, usually juxtapositioned with the Sun. It may symbolise the power of nature. The face represented is that of the Archangel Gabriel, owing to the medieval belief that the moon was his abode.
NAILS: These were used to affix Christ to the cross.
PEACOCK: Symbol of immortality.
PILLAR: Christ was scourged at the pillar.
PINCERS: Tool used for removing the nails from Christ's hands and feet.
SCOURGES: Used to symbolise Christ's suffering.

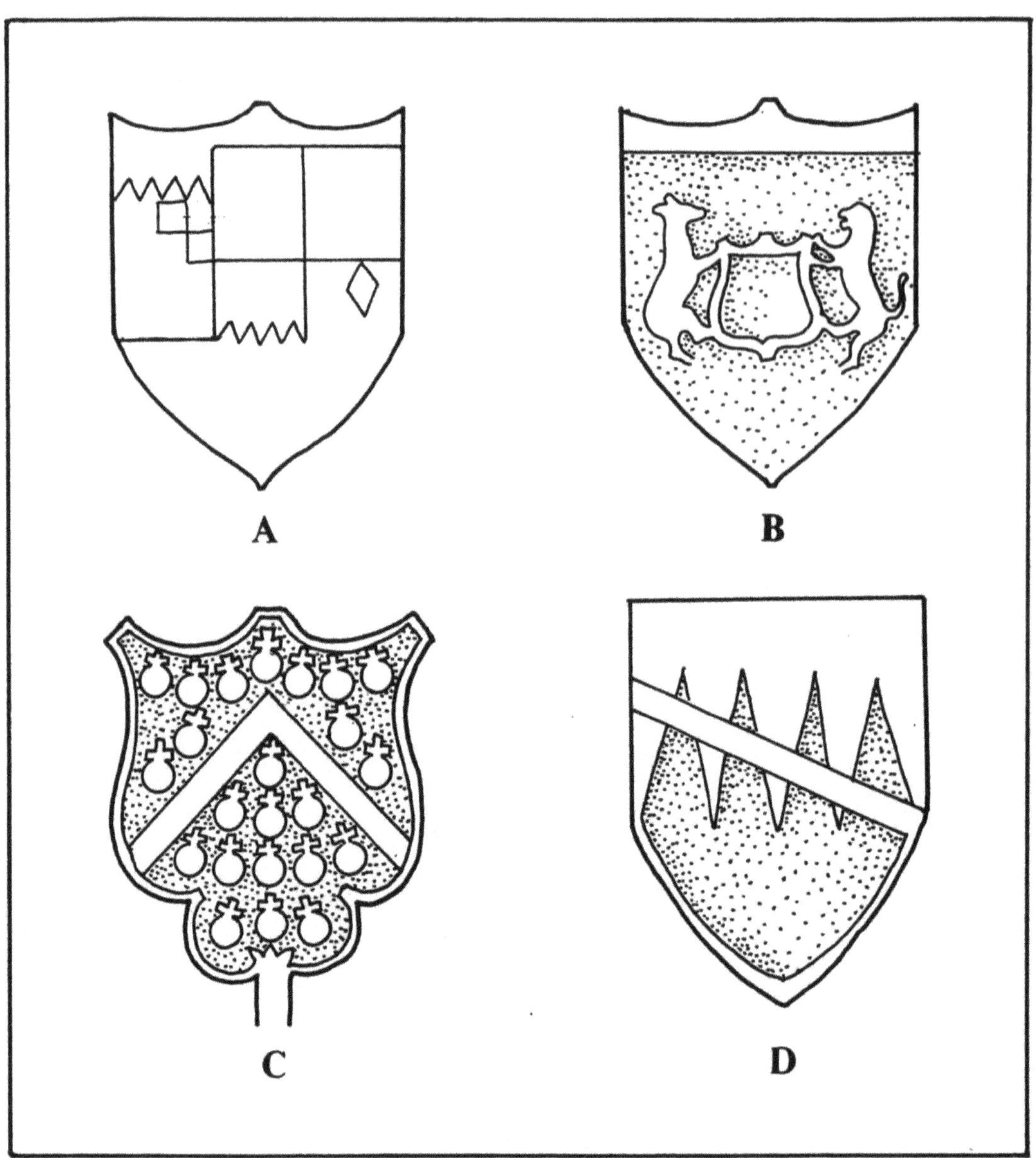

Fig. 17 Heraldic shields from medieval grave-slabs in county Tipperary.

SKULL and CROSS BONES: This symbol of death is often depicted at the foot of the cross. It symbolises victory over death and sin.
SPONGE: Represents the vinegar offered to Christ to drink.
SUN: The symbol of the Resurrection. It is often associated with the moon.
TREE OF LIFE: This can take many forms and represents eternal life.

HERALDRY

Heraldic shields "provide a decorative and attractive display and a permanent symbol of ownership and individuality in a unique and everlasting way and carry the ancient traditions of chivalry, honour and duty" (Oliver 1994, 6). The heraldic shield therefore, serves two purposes: firstly, to illustrate the strong pride in family lineage and, secondly, to aid in making the slab more impressive - a monument of its own with a definite identity.

The origins of heraldry lie in warfare, arising from the warrior's desire to display an emblem in battle. The large surface of the shield provided an increased opportunity for military decoration. These devices were really pre-heraldic as they were not permanent or indicative of lineage. Leaders, knights, the great feudal overlords, church establishments and landowners were amongst those who found it advantageous and necessary to use such recognisable symbols. Therefore heraldic devices were originally used to authenticate documents and instructions by way of seals, and to identify individuals in the press of battle (Oliver 1994, 23).

Heraldic shields occur as secondary emblems on five slabs in Tipperary. Three examples carry bearings: St. Patrick's, Cashel 15 (Fig. 17c) and Fethard Augustinian Abbey 2 and 11 (Fig. 17 a,b;d). One of these, Fethard Abbey 2, may tentatively be identified as that of the Butler family. Old St. Mary's 1 and Fethard Abbey 2 and 3 feature two shields each, one on either side of the cross-shaft. In the case of St. Patrick's 15 the shield overlies the cross-shaft. Heraldry only occurs on a small selection of slabs throughout the country, but more frequently occur on tombs.

ECCLESIASTICAL ICONOGRAPHY

Only one slab in this corpus features ecclesiastical iconography: Kilcooley 3 (Fig. 35). In fact, such iconography is not common among Irish sepulchral monuments in general. However, there are a number of effigies (though not many) which feature ecclesiastical vestments and associated objects, for example those at Kildare Cathedral (Hunt 1974, cat. 87, pl. 69), Kilfenora and Corcomroe, Co. Clare (*ibid*, cat. 10, pl. 77; cat. 2, pl. 74). A typical depiction of the vestments involves a chasuble over an alb, with the hands held either in blessing or in prayer or occasionally holding a book or crozier.

Very often these ecclesiastical figures also feature a pointed mitre. In the case of the Kilcooley 3 example, a figure of an abbot is represented in vestments. He wears a pointed chasuble over a voluminous alb, with IHC inscribed at the bottom. He holds a book in his left hand and has a maniple on his left wrist. In his right hand he holds a large crozier with a foliate head out-turned. The slab dates to 1463 and it is the only example in Tipperary of a slab which features symbols indicative of the career of the person commemorated. It makes an obvious statement - that the abbot was married to his office and it could not be taken from him in death.

MISCELLANEOUS

Liathmore 1 (Fig. 39), which consists of a tapered slab, features a badly worn human figure with out-stretched arms. The figure wears a long robe but there is no indication of nails in his hands. Perhaps it is meant to represent the Triumphant Christ in the manner of the long-robed figures which commonly occurs on twelfth-century high-crosses (Henry 1970, 127-8). It is highly probable that this slab marked the grave of a cleric.

CELTIC REVIVAL MOTIFS

As was already mentioned in Chapter Two, the fifteenth century saw a revival in native culture and language as well as an expansion in architecture. One manifestation of this revival was the revival of Gaelic motifs, such as the 'Celtic' knot and interlace of degenerate form. Such revival motifs can be found in a wide variety of crafts, such as leatherwork, metalwork, manuscripts, stone sculpture etc.

There are only two examples of slabs in Tipperary that display revival characteristics - Lisronagh (Maher 1992, 30-36) and Derrynaflan, (Maher 1994, 162-167). Both slabs, though probably of different dates and of different overall design, do display native aspects.

The Lisronagh slab, for example, features a seven-armed fleur-de-lis cross typical of the sixteenth and early seventeenth centuries. Three 'Celtic' motifs, however, occur in the three surviving sunken segments of the cross-head and in the surviving external spaces between the arms. The motifs include an arrangement of four elongated links with rounded ends which occupies the lower sinister segment of the cross-head (Fig.18 c), an encircled arrangement of a four-legged whirling motif in the upper dexter one (Fig. 18 a), and an irregular lozenge, surrounded by an irregular field, which occupies the lower dexter segment. An incised encircled outline foliate design, which was compass-drawn (Fig. 18 b), occupies the lower dexter external space between the cross-arms. Thus this slab has a mixture of native and Anglo-Norman characteristics, evidence for the latter lying in the form of the seven-armed cross.

Each of the four motifs are 'Celtic' in style and form and they are manifestations of the late medieval revival of interest in native Irish culture, which has been termed the 'Celtic Renaissance'. The four elongated links are a variation of the frequently used duplex motif in late medieval 'Celtic' art. Examples, for instance, occur carved on window embrasures in the churches at Liathmore, Co. Tipperary and Aghadoe, Co. Kerry. A form of the motif occurs in the collection of masons' marks at the Augustinian Abbey, Fethard (Maher 1990, no. 4, Fig. 3). A multi-strand example of this motif occurs on a fifteenth or sixteenth century wooden casket from Co. Clare (Rynne 1971, 39, Pl. 6.3). The Lisronagh motif, like its parallels, should be regarded as a revival of early medieval period duplex knots. Numerous examples of these occur on a series of cross-slabs in the west of Ireland (Higgins 1987, 123, Figs 654 e & d; Wallace and Timoney 1987, 50-51, no's. 4-6). The four-legged whirling motif is also strongly reminiscent of elements of early medieval art. Examples in later contexts occur in the form of decorative ventilators, for example in the tower houses at Coole, Co. Offaly and Derryhivenny, Co. Galway (Leask, 1951, Figs. 60 & 70), and among a range of motifs on a keystone featuring a sheela-na-gig at Ballinderry castle, Co. Galway (Andersen 1977, 144, no. 50). This motif also finds numerous parallels in early medieval carving, metalwork and manuscripts.

The foliate designs, which consist of an arrangement of interlocking almond shaped rings, may be seen as a variation of the marigold motif which frequently occurs on early medieval metalwork and sculpture. A late medieval example occurs in multi-strand form at the head of the mullioned east window at the medieval parish church at Cahir, Co. Tipperary.

Native characteristics are also evident in the Derrynaflan group of head-slabs (Maher 1994, 162-166), especially slab no's 1 and 3. These have already been discussed under the head-slab group in Chapter Three. The features that link them with

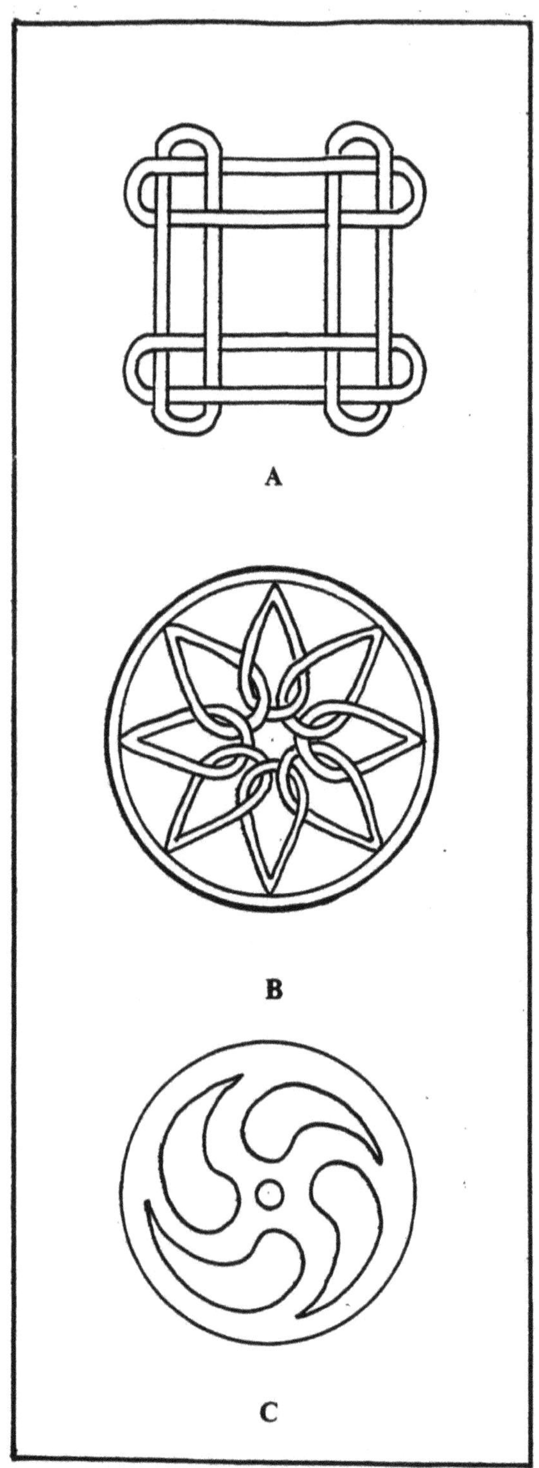

Fig. 18 Celtic revival motifs from the medieval grave-slab at Lisronagh, Co. Tipperary

the classic head-slabs are the cross-heads formed of four penannular circles on slabs no's. 1 and 3, the tapered forms of all three slabs and the presence of the relief heads. On close analysis, however, certain aspects point to a deviation from the classic style. The additional features on slab no.1, for example, do not occur on any other recorded head-slabs. These features include the relief feet at the base of the slab, the circular design formed from four lentoids and the incised human head linked to the base of the enclosing circle. While the basic design can be paralleled with other head-slabs, the overall design is distinctive.

The pair of cross-forms on slab no. 3 are reminiscent of those occurring on some early medieval cross-slabs, for example those at Gallen Priory, Co. Offaly. They also have close affinities to the 'bracelet' cross-form. The above features, along with the poor quality of the stone and the presence of the plain carved human heads, all point to yet another attempt at native revival by the Irish mason.

CHAPTER FIVE

THE INSCRIPTIONS

Nearly fifty per cent of the one hundred and seven slabs in Tipperary bear inscriptions of some form. Thirty-eight of these are in Black Lettering, seven are in Lombardic lettering and only five are in Roman lettering (Fig. 19). The inscriptions invariably occur along the sides of the face of the slab and in a few examples they continue onto the cross shaft or onto the body of the slab, as for example at St. Patrick's, Cashel (no's 6, 19). Preservation of the inscriptions is in most cases sufficiently good to enable at least partial decipherment of them. However, it is not surprising that a number are quite worn and consequently indecipherable, especially when one takes into account their date and location. These latter are often preserved out of doors, in positions where they are subject to weathering, and others serve as thresholds or as floor-slabs. Fortunately, a number of the inscriptions were recorded in the early part of this century and these readings are often of invaluable assistance in modern studies of the inscriptions.

Three main lettering forms occur on Irish medieval grave-slabs: Lombardic, Black Lettering and Roman lettering. The first two types are of greatest relevance to this study. The languages used in the Irish inscriptions include Latin, Norman-French and Irish. In this corpus, however, Latin is predominant.

The Latin alphabet was an important offshoot from the Etruscan one, the adaptation probably taking place in the seventh century B.C. The Romans adapted only twenty-one of the twenty-six Etruscan letters. Several changes and minor alterations took place up to and including the first century B.C. The history of the Latin language after this time consisted of its adaptation to various languages and the transformation of its letters in the cursive styles. From the first century B.C. we also see the use of capitals for both monumental and literary writings. Monumental writings are noted for their evenness, permanence and impressiveness - a point that will be discussed later in this chapter.

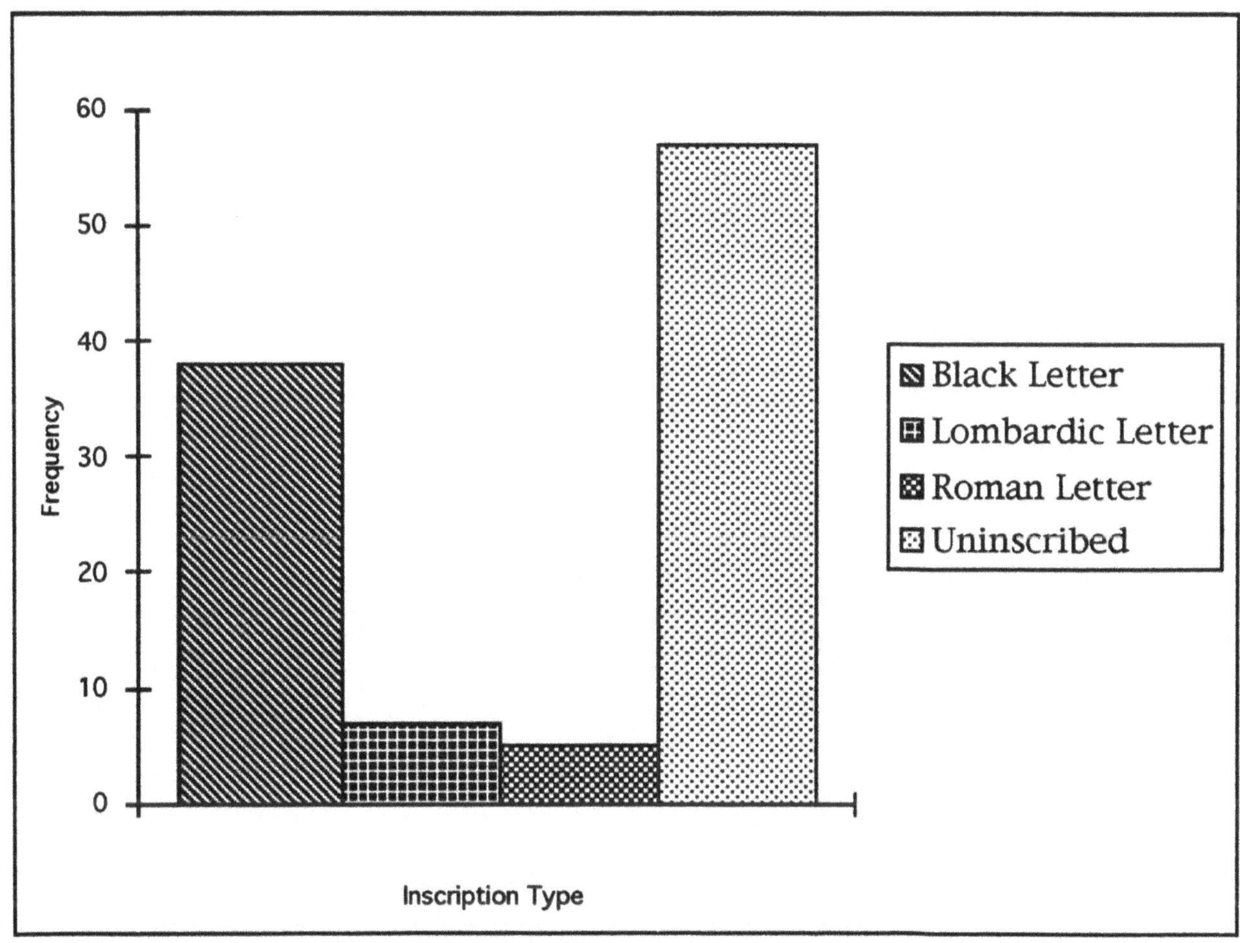

Fig. 19 Bar chart illustrating the numbers of medieval grave-slabs from county Tipperary which are uninscribed or inscribed by letter type.

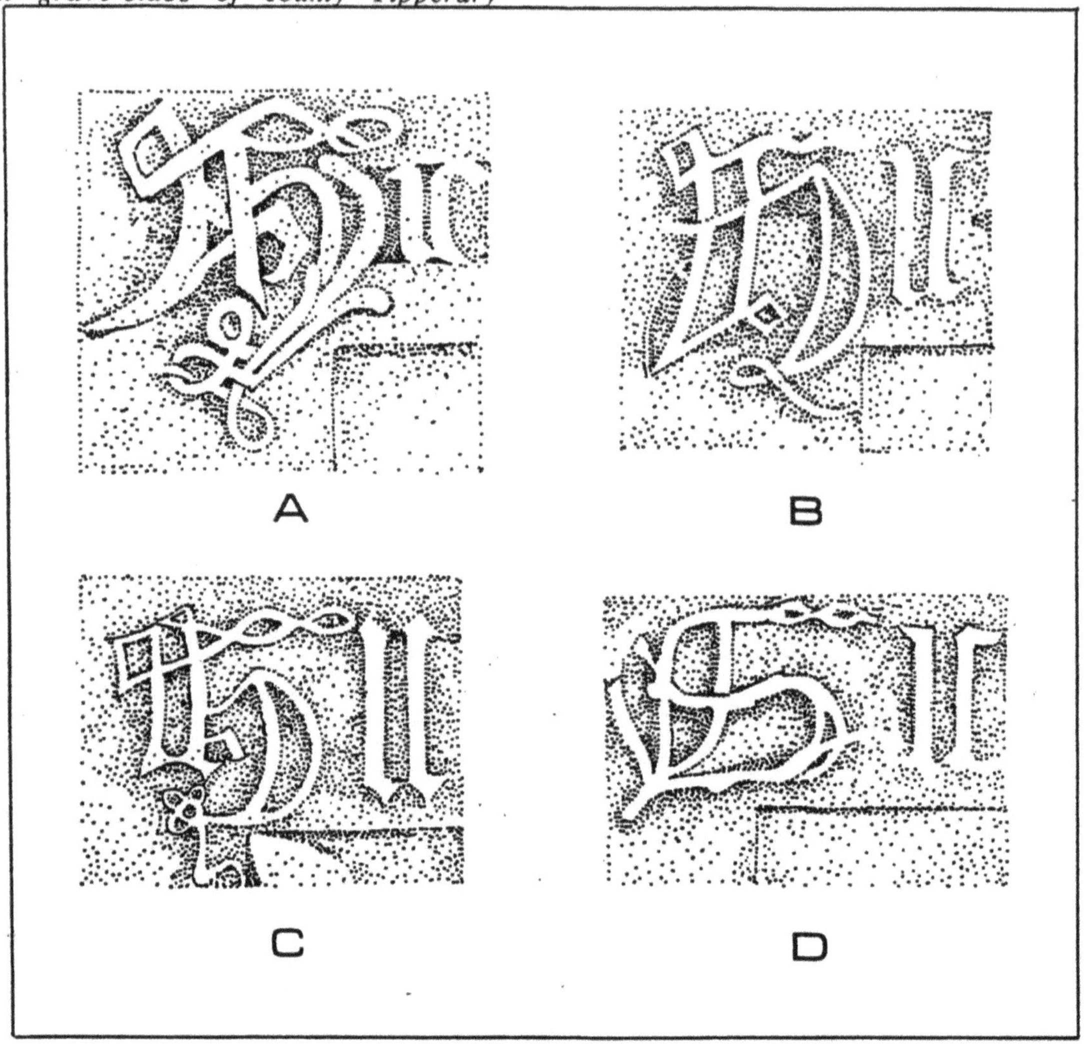

Fig. 20 Examples of decorative initial words (*Hic*) from inscribed grave-slabs from county Tipperary.

A marked change took place in the Latin cursive with the dissolution of the Roman Empire. 'National' styles of writing in the form of cursive minuscule script developed across western Europe. These included, firstly, the Italian semi-cursive minuscule, which was employed throughout Italy from the seventh to the ninth centuries; among its offshoots was the Lombardic minuscule. A second type was the Merovingian script, which was used in France from the sixth to the eighth centuries, while a third was the Visigothic script, which was used in Spain in the eighth and ninth centuries. A fourth was the Germanic pre-Carolingian script, and the fifth comprised the Insular hand, which can be further subdivided into the Celtic and Anglo-Saxon styles.

In the ninth and tenth centuries the Carolingian hand became the principal book-hand in Western Europe. In the twelfth century it developed into localised Frankish, Italian, Germanic and English varieties. A later offshoot from the Carolingian writing was the Black Letter or Gothic script, which was generally employed in north-western Europe until the sixteenth century. One of its main characteristics was its angular shape. German printers took over the Black Letter hand and it became the national hand in Germany after the sixteenth century. There was also the Black Letter round hand, which was an enduring product of Renaissance Italy. This developed into two varieties: the Venetian minuscule (known as italics), and the Roman type of lettering. The typefaces ordinarily used by western printers today developed from these two varieties.

The Latin language and varieties of the Latin script were carried to all parts of western, northern and central Europe. Not surprisingly the national scripts of the majority of European peoples today are adaptations of the Latin alphabet. Even though there may have been a number of modifications, deletions, additions and alterations made to it, in no way has the fundamental structure of the Latin alphabet changed (Diringer 1962, 177).

In this corpus, all of the inscriptions occur in Latin. The main problems which one may encounter in deciphering them include their state of preservation, inaccuracies and illiteracy on the part of the carver and the forms of contractions and abbreviations used in the inscriptions themselves. In fact, the latter features are quite common and occur on virtually every inscribed slab. Examples of words which are quite commonly abbreviated include *QUI, ANNO, DOMINI* and *MENSIS*. The inscription of Kilcooley 2, for example, features many contractions and abbreviations: *HIC IACET JOHANNES CATWELL QUODA DUS DE MOYLASSAIN Q' OBIIT I VIGILA SCI PATRICI A^{O} DO^{O} MO^{O}/CCCCC^{O} XX° II. ET ELICIA STOUC EI' UXOR/RORICUS OTWYNE SCRIPSIT*. The amount of space available for lettering on the grave-slab, along with the length of the required inscription, would obviously be determining factors in the use of abbreviations. However, sheer inaccuracies and/or illiteracy on the part of the stone carver accounts for the misspellings of place-names and of the names of the deceased.

CONTENT OF INSCRIPTIONS

There is a remarkable difference in both content and length between the Lombardic inscriptions and later Black Letter examples. Lombardic inscriptions of the late twelfth to early fourteenth century are short and give little detail. Based on the information as it stands, the main detail supplied is the name of the deceased, in most cases just the Christian name. Athassel 1, for example, reads *HIC IACET FRATER JOH(ANNUS)/JOH(ES)*, which translates as 'Here lies Brother John'. Another slab at Athassel (no. 6) reads *HIC IACET (F?)RA (G/T)ER THOMAS*, which is probably to be interpreted as 'Here lies Brother Thomas'.

Without exception the Lombardic lettering is incised and occurs along the sides of the face of the slab, disposed parallel to the cross, and is generally confined to just one side. However, St. Patrick's Cashel 10 bears a Lombardic inscription which occurs on both long sides.

In the fifteenth and sixteenth centuries Black Lettering became the predominant style. The lettering is now carved in relief - with one exception, Marlfield 2. In the latter case the initial word of the inscription is carved in relief, that is *HIC*, and the remainder of the inscription is incised. This is an interesting feature, firstly because Black Lettering usually occurs in relief and, secondly, because only the first word is in relief. Perhaps this is an unfinished inscription. This point will be discussed later in the chapter.

Black Letter inscriptions are much more elaborate and informative than Lombardic ones: prayers are invoked, surnames as well as Christian names appear and the names of spouses or children are given. Place-names commonly appear, and even the person's rank or position is indicated. The inscription on St. Patrick's 19, for example, is very informative and detailed in this respect. It translates as: 'Here lies Patrick O' Kearney, citizen of Cashel, who died on the 27th day of March [... who was buried?] in the church of Cashel, his body rests before the altar of Brigid, and the tomb which he occupies [...] under the middle stone where they lie he is with Honoria and Patrick Kearney. Now gentle reader, I devoutly beseech you to say for his soul a pater and ave' (Fitzgerald 1903, 438-439). The inscriptions in Black Lettering may occur on both sides of the slab and sometimes extend along the cross-shaft or the slab face. Cashel 4, for example, bears an inscription which occurs on both sides and ends and continues along the cross-shaft, while Cashel 5 bears an inscription on both sides of the cross-shaft.

There is no doubt as to the obvious development in both style and content from the Lombardic inscriptions of the late twelfth to fourteenth centuries to the Black Letter inscriptions of the late fourteenth to sixteenth centuries. Grave-slabs with Black Letter inscriptions in the later centuries are far more common than slabs with Lombardic inscriptions in the earlier centuries. This fact could be seen as a consequence of the introduction of printing and of the greater circulation of printed books in the sixteenth century. So, this increase in the number of slabs bearing inscriptions might be taken as reflection of social and cultural aspects of the period.

Another aspect of this style of lettering which does not feature in the Lombardic script is its sense of permanence, evenness and impressiveness. This can be viewed as one part of the overall development of grave-slabs at this time. In the sixteenth century especially we see a manifestation of this development. The large rectangular slabs, perfectly finished, with elaborate crosses carved in relief and elaborate detailed inscriptions, together played an important part in the commemoration of socially significant people.

A decorative feature which is worthy of note is the initial letter of the Black Letter inscriptions. '*H* " is the dominant initial letter, as most inscriptions commence with '*HIC JACET*'. There are a number of examples of the initial letter being elaborated in an interlaced fashion: for example, St. Patrick's, Cashel 4, 16 and 17 (Fig. 20b,c,d), Old St. Mary's, Clonmel 1 (Fig. 20a) and Holycross 7. On examination of the designs and inscriptions which feature on medieval grave-slabs, it becomes clear that the production of such memorials was not an isolated phenomenon. It must be viewed as evidence for the awareness by the grave-slab producers of contemporary developments in architecture and the arts. In the context of this chapter, for example, an awareness of contemporary manuscripts is implied, as these are an obvious source for the decorative initial letters of the slabs. The sole purpose of the initial letter in manuscripts is that of decoration. The same can be applied to those elaborate initial letters on grave-slabs. Decorative initials were normal in printed books for several centuries, and there is a continuous history of the illuminated initial in medieval manuscripts. Contemporary Irish medieval manuscripts - for example, the fourteenth-century *Book of Ballymote*, the fifteenth-century *Book of Lecan, The Book of Lismore* and the sixteenth-century *Leabhar Breac* - all provide a great variety of forms in the use of the

Fig. 21 Detail of inscription and adjacent prepared surface on a sixteenth century tomb at Kilcooley, Co. Tipperary.

Fig. 22 Detail of unfinished inscription on Marlfield 2, Co. Tipperary.

initial letter. While there are no recorded exact parallels between the initial letters of manuscripts and those of grave-slabs, there is little doubt that the former provided the stone carver with many decorative ideas.

METHOD OF INSCRIBING

The consistent and accurate spacings and measurements of the Black Letter inscription, together with its regularity and evenness, suggest that there was a careful approach to inscribing it. One possible method involves three stages: firstly, the spacings for the individual letters were laid out; secondly, the forms of the letters were incised, and, finally, the background was removed to leave the letters in relief. This proposed sequence is based on a study of two slabs, one from Kilcooley Abbey and the other from Marlfield.

On a tomb in Kilcooley, set in the north wall of the chancel (Hunt 1974, cat. 243, pl. 151), a number of incised lines occur on the dexter side of the covering slab (Fig. 21). They occur at the end of a Black Letter inscription and cover an area measuring .70m in length. They consist of two longitudinally incised lines, which are set .02m apart. The first .18m of the panel bears incised vertical lines, which are regularly spaced at 6mm intervals. The upper longitudinal line occurs at the same level as the tops of the inner voids of the adjacent lettering. The thickness of the adjacent lettering corresponds to the spacing between the incised vertical lines, which is also 6mm. It may be assumed that this was the first stage - laying out the spacing for the letters - of preparing a surface for a Black Letter inscription.

As is mentioned above, the first word of the Black Letter inscription on Marlfield 2 is in relief, the remainder being incised (Fig. 22). Because of the unique nature of this arrangement it is almost certain that it is an unfinished slab. This is an example of the proposed second stage in the method of inscribing, that is the incision of the letters. The third proposed stage is the removal of the background, thus leaving the letters in relief. Unfortunately we lack other evidence for methods of inscribing.

CHAPTER SIX

DISTRIBUTION AND DEVELOPMENT

Unfortunately, it is not feasible to formulate a meaningful typology of Tipperary's medieval grave-slabs. Not only is the geographical study area too confined in extent, but the overall development of medieval grave-slabs cannot necessarily be regarded as a progressive one. A considerable amount of diversity in design occurs within each century of the period. A number of distinct localised groups, nevertheless, were identified during the course of the research, but these pose difficulties in the formation of a typology. Certain distinctions in the design and form of the grave-slabs over the centuries are, however, evident. The purpose of this chapter is to outline and discuss the development of the slabs from the twelfth-early thirteenth century until the end of the sixteenth century. The distribution patterns of the slabs during each century will also be addressed. It should also be noted at this point that this discussion is based on eighty-five out of the total of one hundred and seven slabs, as seven of the remaining twenty-two remain unclassifiable and fifteen do not bear designs.

TWELFTH-EARLY THIRTEENTH CENTURY

Grave-slabs of this period are poorly represented in Tipperary, with only five recorded examples: Baptist Grange 1, Coolmundry 1, Kiltinan 1 and 2 and Liathmore 1. The first four examples have already been discussed as a distinct local group which centres on the area north of Clonmel and has no parallels elsewhere in the country (see Chapter Three). There are only two features which the remaining slab, Liathmore 1, and the other four have in common: they are all of sandstone and are tapered in form. Unfortunately, none of the slabs features dates or inscriptions and they all bear different designs. These vary from the Christ-like figure raised in relief on Liathmore 1 to the subcircular cross-head with three short arms surmounting a cross-stem formed of three grooves on, for example, Coolmundry 1. The twelfth to thirteenth century date suggested for these slabs is based on a number of features, such as the volutes on Kiltinan 2, the possible early medieval cross-head influence on the design of Coolmundry 1 and the carved human figure with its long robe on Liathmore 1. Each of these features have parallels with other Irish stone carvings of this date, such as the Clare and Aran high-crosses (see Chapter Three).

Overall the grave-slabs of this period (in Tipperary at any rate) cannot be grouped on the basis of a unifying cross-type. It is possible, in fact, that they, with their essentially native characteristics, date to before the Anglo-Norman period. An obvious outside influence, however, is their tapered form, and this would suggest that they date to after the arrival of the Anglo-Normans.

THIRTEENTH-EARLY FOURTEENTH CENTURY

Grave-slabs of this period in Tipperary are only represented by sixteen examples, occurring in Holycross, Holy Trinity Church, Fethard, Donaghmore, Kilcooley, St. Patrick's Cathedral, Cashel, Derrynaflan, St Dominick's, Cashel and Two-Mile-Borris. The slabs at these sites include examples from Groups 1, 3 and 5. There is no apparent connection with the slabs of the preceding period nor, indeed, is there any evidence of influence or development from one type to the other. Only one of the slabs is of sandstone - Donaghmore 2. Fifteen slabs are tapered, five of them feature chamfered edges but only two slabs - St. Patrick's Cathedral, Cashel 1 and St Dominick's, Cashel 7 - feature an inscription (both in Lombardic lettering). Three examples - Holycross 2, 3 and 4 - have no surviving design and these are only tentatively assigned to this period, based on their form. Holycross 5, which consists of the lower portion of a tapered slab with chamfered edges, features an incised outline cross-shaft which terminates in a trefoil base. Holy Trinity 2 consists of the lower portion of a tapered slab and it also features an incised outline cross-stem terminating in a trefoil. The latter two slabs can only be tentatively assigned to this period, as only the base of their design survives. The remaining eleven slabs - though they each feature different designs - do share a number of features, however, and they also have close affinities with certain English examples. Five of these - Derrynaflan 1, 2 and 3, St. Patrick's, Cashel 1, and Two-Mile-Borris 1 - are head-slabs (see Chapter Three). Derrynaflan 2 only features a carved human head, while Derrynaflan 3, which survives in two portions, features two examples. Due to the fragmentary nature of the latter slab, however, the upper portion of the incised outline design does not survive fully. The design on its lower portion consists of two encircled 'bracelet' crosses (a cross formed of four penannular circles). This and each of the other head-slabs - with the exception of Two-Mile-Borris 1 - are tapered and feature cruciform designs akin to Ryder's 'bracelet cross-form' (1985, 9-10), a design which is dated to the thirteenth century in Britain. There are also a number of features which are unique to each of these slabs: for example, St. Patrick's, Cashel 1 is the only slab from this group to feature a Lombardic inscription and chamfered edges. Its cross terminates in a stepped base, while Derrynaflan 1 features carved 'feet' as its cross-base. Two-Mile-Borris 1 features a pointed top, which is quite an uncommon feature amongst medieval grave-slabs. As was pointed out in

Chapter Three, the Tipperary head-slabs appear to form a degenerate group, a cul-de-sac development of its own, which, while stemming from the 'classic' head-slab of Anglo-Norman type, features a combination of native and non-native influences.

Two other grave-slabs assigned to this period are Donaghmore 2 and Kilcooley 4. Both of these are also akin to the 'bracelet' cross-form: Donaghmore 2 is a tapered, chamfered sandstone slab and features a cruciform design formed of four penannular circles set in a sunken circle; Kilcooley 4 features a cruciform motif formed of eight penannular circles and could be classed as a 'bracelet' derivative form. This slab is also tapered and features chamfered edges.

The four remaining slabs which may be assigned to this period comprise St. Dominick's, Cashel 1, 2, 7 and 9. These have already been discussed in Chapter Three and are of Group 5 type. no's 1, 2 and 9 each feature an incised outline cross which terminates in a large trefoil. St. Dominick's 7 is unusual in that the design it features consists simply of an incised outline stem with a trefoil at each end. Each of these slabs is unique, with their closest parallels occurring in England. There are some similarities evident, however, between their style of carving and some of the Athassel slabs. Based on these similarities, and on the dated parallels with the English slabs, they can be assigned to the thirteenth or fourteenth centuries.

It is only in the thirteenth and early fourteenth century period that diagnostic cross-types begin to emerge in Tipperary - that is the 'bracelet' cross-form and the simple, incised, floriated crosses. Their influence is essentially English, though native influences are also apparent in the former group. The number of grave-slabs known from Tipperary during this period is quite low, but this may simply be due to the fact that they were re-used for building purposes or became buried over time. Secondly, it may be that the practice of carving grave-slabs in Tipperary was not as firmly established at this time as it was in more heavily colonised areas, such as Wexford and Kilkenny. It is clear from the considerations of the designs on the above slabs that, while there is evidence for the employment of introduced cross-types, there is also a large number of individual and unparalleled features occurring on them. This, presumably, is a consequence of the tenuous nature of the Anglo-Norman settlement in Tipperary. In terms of their distribution, all of the thirteenth and early fourteenth century slabs in Tipperary are found in the south of the county east of the River Suir - the area which was most heavily affected by the Anglo-Norman colonisation.

FOURTEENTH CENTURY

As is the case for the preceding periods, there is no grave-slab from Tipperary from this period which actually carries a dated inscription. Therefore, the slabs dealt with in this section are only tentatively assigned to this century. These comprise eight examples, located at Athassel, Ardmayle, Marlfield and Holycross. With the exception of the Marlfield example, these slabs are all located in mid and west Tipperary. Six of the slabs located at the first two sites are of Group 5 type and have already been discussed in Chapter Three. Each of these feature different outline designs, though they also have a number of features in common. Firstly, they all feature an incised cross with some form of floriated/trefoil terminals and, in most cases, they are richly decorated (Fig.14 m-p). Secondly, most of them feature an outline circle beneath the cross-head which surmounts a narrow cross-stem terminating in a single trefoil. It is suggested that Ardmayle1 and Athassel 1, 2, 8, 9 and 11 were the products of one school of carvers; this is apparent because of the similarities outlined above and also because of the similar execution of design of the small trefoil motifs at their arm terminals and the larger ones at their cross-bases. Although the cross-head designs of the slabs from St. Dominick's, Cashel, are essentially different to those of the Athassel and Ardmayle group, there are a number of comparable features. These include the style of execution of the design, the use of the outline incised circle beneath the cross-head, the use of the circle enclosing the cross-head and the similarities between the single-lobed stems of St. Dominick's 9 and Athassel 2.

Based on the above similarities, there is no reason to doubt that the slabs from Athassel, Ardmayle and St. Dominick's Abbey, Cashel, are all of the same general period and are probably of fourteenth century date. This proposed date is based primarily on parallels drawn between these slabs and English examples, since none of the Tipperary examples are dated. Only one of the above slabs features an inscription, St. Dominick's 7, and this is in Lombardic lettering.

The remaining two slabs, which are also only tentatively assigned to this period, comprise Holycross 10 and Marlfield 1. The latter features a Lombardic inscription and its design consists of an incised, outline, straight-armed cross with four simple trefoils at the terminals. The cross-head surmounts a narrow cross-stem which terminates in a stepped base. Holycross 10 also features an incised, outline, straight-armed cross with trefoils at each arm terminal, similar to those of Marlfield 1. The base of the design does not survive, nor is there any trace of an inscription. These two slabs more than likely belong to the early to mid-fourteenth century rather than to an earlier period, as they do not feature the prominent taper and chamfer of slabs of the preceding centuries. Secondly, the stepped base is more commonly found on slabs of the fourteenth century. Finally, there are a few examples in Ryder's collection of grave-slabs from Durham which feature a similar design, for example Barnard Castle, St. Mary's, no's 8 and 12 (1985, 55), and these he assigns to this period.

Based on the recorded examples from Tipperary county, there is no single cross-type that can be assigned to the fourteenth-century period. Rather, a number of new forms appear consisting of both the seven-armed and three-armed types. The typical fleur-de-lis, which was common on thirteenth and fourteenth century grave-slabs from elsewhere in the country - for example Wexford and Kilkenny - was not, however, a feature of the fourteenth century Tipperary slabs. Instead, a simple trefoil or a large three-lobed motif feature at the arm terminals and cross-base. Overall these slabs, which are invariably tapered, display richness and variety in design. There is very little overlap in the designs between the thirteenth and fourteenth centuries, except, perhaps, in the from of the cross-bases of Holy Trinity 2 and Holycross 5. Influences and parallels with Britain, especially south western England, become even more apparent during this period.

FIFTEENTH CENTURY

Fifteenth century grave-slabs are the least represented of all in county Tipperary, with only two dated examples - Kilcooley 3 and 6. Lisronagh 1 and Donaghmore 1, however, may also be assigned to this period. The distribution of these slabs is not coherent, with examples occurring at one site in north Tipperary - Kilcooley - and at two sites in the south east - Donaghmore and Lisronagh.

Each of the four slabs feature different designs and include some of the most interesting and significant features in this corpus. Such features range from the symbols of the passion to 'Celtic' motifs and the figure of an abbot carved in false relief. Kilcooley 3 and 6 are the only Tipperary grave-slabs known to feature a selection of the symbols of the passion. The latter slab is dated by inscription to 1452. It does not feature a cross-head as the Crown of Thorns, which is suspended from the Cup and Lance, takes its place. The symbols of the passion, which occupy the upper portion of the slab, surmount its cross-shaft, which terminates in a stepped base. This is the only example of a stepped base in this period. Kilcooley 3 is also a grave-slab of some significance, not only because of the passion symbols it features but also because it carries the figure of an abbot. This figure, carved in false relief, occupies the lower portion of the slab and is surmounted by the *arma christi*. It is dated by inscription to 1463. This slab and Kilcooley 6 are the earliest recorded examples of slabs in the county to feature a Black Letter inscription. The style of the carving of the figure on Kilcooley 3 is typical of this period. However, the presence of such a figure on medieval cross-slabs is unique. The only other example of a grave-slab within the county to feature a carved human figure is the twelfth-early thirteenth century slab at Liathmore.

Lisronagh 1 is tentatively assigned to this period, based on its 'Celtic' affinities. Unfortunately, a good portion of the top and upper sinister corner of the slab is broken off, though the remains of a seven-armed cross survive. Overall the slab is richly decorated, with each of the surviving external spaces and the three surviving internal segments of the cross-head featuring a number of 'Celtic' and vegetal-like motifs (Maher 1992, 30-37).

Perhaps one of the more obvious reasons for the decline in Anglo-Norman sculpture during the mid to late fourteenth century and right through the fifteenth century was the disastrous effects of the Black Death of 1348-49. In the following century the preoccupation of the English with the War of the Roses allowed the Irish and the Old English to revive their fortunes. This period of resurgence saw the revival of Gaelic culture and language. It also saw the revival of Celtic motifs, evident in the array of mason's marks at Fethard Augustinian Abbey and also at Kilcooley, Hore Abbey and Holycross (Stalley 1987, 43, fig. 6-8; Maher 1990, 35-41). The Gaelic revival also manifested itself in the Celtic interlace knots which are visible on the window-spandrels of many tower houses of this period. This revival was not just confined to stonework, but it was also evident in the metalwork of the period, for example the Ballylongford Cross, which was commissioned for John O'Connor, Lord of Kerry, in 1479. While the cross-head which features on Lisronagh 1 was to become the typical sixteenth century cross-type, its motifs and their cultural and political significance makes this slab all the more interesting and important. Unfortunately, no other such slab has been recorded in Tipperary.

The only other slab which is assigned to this period is Donaghmore 1. No inscription or date occurs on it, and its proposed date is based on stylistic grounds. It is only slightly tapered and features a small chamfer. It is decorated by a straight-armed cross, carved in relief, terminating in a pillar-base form. The single cross-bands, which occur on each arm acting as a 'collar' to the simple trefoil terminals, along with the cross-bands at the top and base of the shaft, together with the style of the base of the cross and the style of the overall carving, places this slab in the late medieval bracket. It is not typical of the richly floriated, outline, incised grave-slabs of the preceding period, nor is it related to the sixteenth century examples which so often feature the common seven-armed fleur-de-lis cross with a base akin to a pillar-base.

It is clear that as well as fifteenth century grave-slabs being very poorly represented in the county, there is no identifiable cross-type assignable to this period. Rather it is a century, yet again, marked by variation. There is no obvious progression from the fourteenth to the fifteenth century apparent in the slabs, nor is there any major evidence of outside influences. This is especially the case since the symbols of the passion were more common among Irish medieval grave-slabs than they were among English examples, and the presence of the 'Celtic' motifs is essentially an insular feature.

SIXTEENTH CENTURY

Sixteenth-century grave-slabs are more numerous in Tipperary than those of any other century, with approximately forty examples on record. The sixteenth century also has the largest percentage of dated slabs in Tipperary. It is possible to identify a predominant cross-type in this period, that is the seven-armed fleur-de-lis cross (Fig.14 q-s). These slabs are well represented throughout the county. Examples occur at Loughmore and Lorrha in the north, Kilcooley in the north east, Holycross and Cashel in mid-Tipperary and Fethard and Clonmel in the south.

The main attribute of these slabs is their impressive size, with some examples being up to 2m in length. This imbues them with a sense of permanence, while their elaborate carved designs, along with the widely used Black Letter inscriptions, also combine to contribute to the overall impressiveness of these types of slabs. Usually they are of rectangular shape and in some cases it is possible to identify them as tomb lids (see Chapter Three). In all cases the design is in relief, except for Loughmore 1 where it is partly incised and partly in relief. The other main attribute of these slabs, apart from the typical cross-type, is the raised border which occurs around the margins of the slab face. This frequently carries a Black Letter inscription. The seven-armed fleur-de-lis cross was also in vogue elsewhere in the country, where other cross-forms were also represented.

While the seven-armed cross is the sixteenth-century design *par excellence*, other cross-types also occur in Tipperary, for example the unusual cross carved on Old St. Mary's, Clonmel 1. This consists of a straight-armed ringed cross with bifid terminals. Four further arms, with expanded terminals occur at the angles of the cross-head, which surmounts a fluted shaft with an elaborate pillar-base form. The slab features two dates, 1583 and 1592, and is the only dated sixteenth century slab from the county which does not feature the seven-armed cross-form.

The obvious question to be considered at this stage is why there was a remarkable increase in the number of grave-slabs being carved in the county during the sixteenth century? During this period a number of debilitating events took place, such as the dissolution of the monasteries which Hunt regarded as helping to "bring about the decline of the now almost traditional armoured effigies in the Fitzgerald lands" (1974, 12). It is, therefore, surprising that there should be a boom in grave-slab production in the county whilst political and ecclesiastical strife was rampant. However, on the other hand, this period also saw an increase in the construction of tower houses. Perhaps this breakdown of the feudal system not only resulted in a determination to defend, by building tower houses, but also in a determination to carry on reinforcing identity and power - an identity and power which the funerary monuments were intended to convey to future generations. Is the impressiveness and unageing aspect of these sixteenth-century monuments a reflection of the society of which they were part?

In conclusion, it should be quite clear at this stage that a definitive typology of medieval grave-slabs within county Tipperary is, as has been pointed out above, difficult to formulate. It is possible, however, to outline a general development for this monument type over the centuries, that is a development from the recumbent grave-slab, which is distinctly tapered and features a prominent chamfer, bearing a simple incised cross, to the later, larger, rectangular or slightly tapered slabs, featuring elaborate crosses carved in relief. There is also a development evident in the inscriptions - a progressive development from the short Lombardic inscriptions which contain little detail to the larger and longer Black Letter inscriptions (see Chapter Five).

Following the above account of grave-slab design and form for each century, one of the most significant and interesting factors to emerge is the diversity of design evident in each of them, except perhaps in the sixteenth century. Evidence for both external and native influences are detectable in the designs. This, in itself, is an interesting reflection of contemporary society. As well as the diversity in design, a number of local groups are identifiable - grouped according to cross-head type and certain stylistic features - which suggests that they are the products of a single carver or a school of carvers. The main problem with the grave-slabs, from the twelfth/thirteenth century right up to the fifteenth century, is the absence of exact dating evidence and the small numbers of surviving examples. In these cases only tentative dates can be suggested on the basis of parallels abroad or with other types of stonework in Ireland, for example carved effigies, late high crosses and tombs. For a true picture of the development of grave-slabs in Ireland a larger sample is required. Then the actual extent of the diversity of design would, hopefully, become evident and a larger number of localised groups of slabs would probably be identified.

CHAPTER SEVEN

CONCLUSIONS

One purpose of this study is to measure the contribution a study of medieval grave-slabs can have towards the study of the reality of the past, or as Crossley notes, how it helps us "to visualise the life, aspirations, religious emotions and artistic impulses" of medieval people (1921, 18). Gillespie has indicated that "an understanding of funeral monuments can lead to an understanding of the values and priorities of a society and not just its religious beliefs" (1992, 8). A study of the medieval grave-slabs of Tipperary, while of interest and value in itself, must also assess the broad social significance of this material. This may be achieved by examining various aspects of the slabs, including their inscriptions, the simplicity or complexity of their design, the presence of additional symbols and motifs and their exact location.

Inscriptions and epitaphs are an obvious but important source. The common function of all epitaphs is identification, and one important piece of information they sometimes provide is the type of people commemorated. The following proper-nouns are quite common among the Tipperary inscriptions: *Vir*, *Dominus*, *Frater*, *Abbas*, *Magister* and *Rector*, and these suggest that grave-slabs were commissioned for people of the higher social strata in the majority of cases. Among those commemorated were the high ranking ecclesiastics, wealthy merchants and landowners. This is evidenced by the occurrence of the surnames of wealthy landowners and merchants at the time - for example Fogarty in Holycross, Kearny in Cashel, and Meagher and Everard in Fethard - and it is these names and those of others in similar capacities that are inscribed on many of these grave-slabs.

Words like 'elaborate', 'permanence' and 'powerful' have been frequently used throughout this work in reference to the Tipperary grave-slabs. It should also be pointed out that there is direct evidence from the inscriptions of a number of sixteenth-century slabs that these were sometimes commissioned during the lifetimes of those commemorated, for example Fethard Augustinian Abbey 11 and the Peter Butler slab in Wexford (Garstin 1899, 321). Perhaps the most interesting Irish example of this type of forward planning occurs at Gowran church, Co. Kilkenny (Hunt 1974, cat. 104 and 105; pl. 31 and 32), where two effigies survive - the first is probably that of James le Butler and the second appears to be that of Eleanor de Bohun, his wife. Hunt notes that after the death of her first husband, James le Butler, she married Sir Thomas de Dagworth in 1344. As the above two effigies form a pair, it is likely that they were both carved at the same time, and before James' death and Eleanor's second marriage. Gillespie makes reference to another similar example, noting how "Sir Arthur Chichester, while stipulating in his will that his funeral would be decent and convenient, had ensured before his death that a large monument was erected over the vault to perpetuate the name" (1985, 89). This occurred in the seventeenth century, but no doubt was a reflection of funerary practices in previous centuries.

From these examples alone it is obvious that to be remembered after death was considered to have been of importance amongst the late medieval wealthy classes. In fact, the urge to be remembered is as old as man himself, and implies a *multa mei vitabit libitinam* attitude among the socially significant classes. Even though Horace was referring to his literature with these words, they are still applicable here. This strong concern to be remembered after death is not just manifested in medieval grave-slabs and their inscriptions, but is also obvious in the very elaborate tombs and effigies of the same period. Ariès, in considering the epitaph, stated that it became "the most common means for men of the Middle Ages to emerge from anonymity and acquire a tomb that was specifically their own" (1985, 40). Ironically this whole idea was used as satire by Shelley in the sonnet *Ozymandias*, in which he depicts the futility of "the boast of heraldry, the pomp of power". On the other hand Yeats believed in the immortality of art "monuments of unageing intellect" and in the idea that the liberated spirit (in art) "will sing of what is past, present and to come". This preoccupation with recording identity in death is not surprising when one considers the attitudes and lifestyles of important medieval people.

When one views all medieval sepulchral monuments together, including effigies, tombs, cadaver monuments and grave-slabs, a "civilization of individual identity" where "men retained in death the particular characteristics that had distinguished them in life" (Ariès 1985, 31) becomes apparent.

One of the principal points that becomes apparent from a study of the Tipperary slabs is that the cross-forms present on most of them are related to those on British slabs. Similarly, the tapered forms of many of the earlier slabs owe their origins to Anglo-Norman styles. These slabs may, therefore, be regarded as monumental representations of the consciously cultural distinctiveness of the new settlers. It can be argued that as the slabs carry connotations of supremacy and permanence - with their elaborate crosses, inscriptions and, sometimes, heraldic motifs - they also acted as devices which served to identify the newcomers with medieval Tipperary and rooted them into its landscape.

Despite the fact that some of the medieval slabs from Tipperary carry inscriptions which identify them with native families, such as the O'Meagher slabs in Fethard (no's 9 and 11), it is, nonetheless, striking that the vast majority of them occur in the heavily colonised southern and eastern parts of the county (Fig. 23). This distribution pattern reinforces the identification of these slabs with the Anglo-Norman families and their descendants. It could be argued, however, that some of the native families in this area, such as the aforementioned O"Meaghers, survived the conquest to become integrated with the Anglo-Normans, though it is clear from the historical sources that the major native septs in this area disintegrated completely (Empey 1985, 87). In this way the medieval slabs may be viewed as evidence for the complexity of the composition of Tipperary society.

This complexity is further underlined when the Gaelic resurgence within the county is considered. The historical sources tell us that this resurgence only took place in those areas of the county, such as the north, which had not been heavily colonised (Empey 1985, 88-89). However, the archaeological evidence may serve to mellow this view somewhat. Grave-slabs with Celtic revival motifs are confined in their distribution to the south of the county - such as at Lisronagh (Maher 1992, 30-37) and Derrynaflan (Maher 1994, 162-66) - and related motifs, such as the fine collection of masons' marks at the Augustinian Abbey, Fethard (Maher 1990, 35-41), are also found in other contexts there. In the north of the county, where the Gaelic resurgence was most pronounced, the Celtic revival is not represented on funerary monuments at all. Perhaps the evidence from the south represents a cultural renewal by the suppressed Gaelic families there. In a sense this represents a conscious process of symbolic identification - perhaps a proclamation - by the Gaelic families which echoes that indulged in by the Anglo-Normans in the early stages of the conquest.

Another interesting point which is worthy of note is the attitude to death of people in the Middle Ages. Does this attitude influence the form of sepulchral carving in any way? Reference has already been made to the words *Memento Mori* inscribed across the base of Old St. Mary's 2. Even though there is only one example of this in Tipperary, it is still of significance. According to the medieval theology of St. Augustine, all human actions were *sub specie aeternitatis* (under the eye of eternity). This doctrine must have had a profound influence on the social strata in the Middle Ages, evidence for which lies in the numerous emblems and symbols carved on the grave-slabs. Therefore, a study of iconography not only provides us with an insight into the medieval artisan, but also into the religious attitudes of the period. Roe notes how literature in the fifteenth and sixteenth centuries contained many allusions to the universality of death, and how these obsessions find expression in contemporary paintings - for example the *Dance of Death* (1968, 1, 2). Bleak inscriptions carved on tombs to remind man of his mortality were not uncommon, one of the more spectacular occurring on the sixteenth century Ronan memorial in Cork - "Be mindful o man since death tarries not; for when thou diest, thou shalt inherit serpents, beasts and worms" (*ibid* 1968, 2). Perhaps *Memento Mori* is an adaptation from an extract of the liturgy on Ash Wednesday, originating in the middle ages - *Memento homo, cineres es et in cinerem reverteris* (Remember man thou art but dust and into dust thou shalt return).

The above quotations and medieval doctrines illustrate the medieval concept of death and its influence on contemporary lifestyles. The production of medieval sepulchral monuments, complete with epitaphs of identification, the "boast of heraldry", the *arma christi* and its overall aspiration to art as eternal, was obviously not just a consequence of mere sculpting, but also a consequence of the contemporary social norms of the day.

If one views the grave-slabs in a political context, however, other interesting questions and issues arise. From the mid-sixteenth century onwards, for example, a series of Acts of Parliament were passed extirpating Catholic usage and imagery in both England and Ireland. Therefore, when we see the symbols of the passion, in all their entirety, carved on Irish sepulchral monuments are we looking at a deliberate refusal by certain people to conform to such acts? Surely this is not a question of mere politics, but also one of strong religious beliefs and an equally strong preoccupation with the afterlife.

Probably one of the most curious and interesting details which was specific to an individual, and raises questions, occurs in the early sixteenth century inscription of St. Patrick's Cathedral 5. Along the sinister side of the shaft the following is inscribed: *ROBERTUS HACKETT ARCH' DACON' CASSELIE. INTESTATUS DECESSIT DECEM DIE DECEMBRIS* (Robert Hackett Archdeacon of Cashel, died intestate on the tenth of December). Obviously the interesting word is 'intestate'; was this so important to the family that they had to carve it on his tombstone? Did it cause a family feud and this was their way of getting their revenge? However, the real answers to such questions might never be known, but the important point regarding this issue is the way it presents the grave-slab not merely as a record of identity, or an appeal for prayer directed to the passerby, but also in some cases as a type of biography.

In Chapter Three references were made to the existence of styles and schools of carving in the county. there appears to be a relationship between these with particular types of ecclesiastical sites. For instance, slabs with native characteristics tend to occur at parish church sites, while slabs at major monastic sites and cathedrals - for example those at

Kilcooley, Holycross and Cashel - display relationships with one another which may emphasise the significance of the role of patronage on medieval carvers. The form of some slabs also indicate the likelihood of the presence of foreign carvers in Tipperary: the fourteenth century Athassel slabs, for instance, display such a close degree of similarity with certain examples in south and south-west England that they may well be the work of English carvers. Unfortunately, only one Tipperary carver is named in the corpus of inscriptions: this is Rory O'Tunney, the sixteenth-century maker of Kilcooley 2, whose work is to be found throughout counties Tipperary and Kilkenny.

In conclusion each slab has a statement to make, be it political, social or religious. They also have a function - anything from perpetuation of identity to an enduring request for prayers for the souls of the deceased. Gillespie's comments on the funeral in seventeenth century Ireland may also be applied to the preceding centuries - it was "a crucial institution in.... Ireland providing an occasion both for the demonstration of the status of the deceased and a public demonstration of the passage of land from one generation to another" (1985, 90).

CATALOGUE

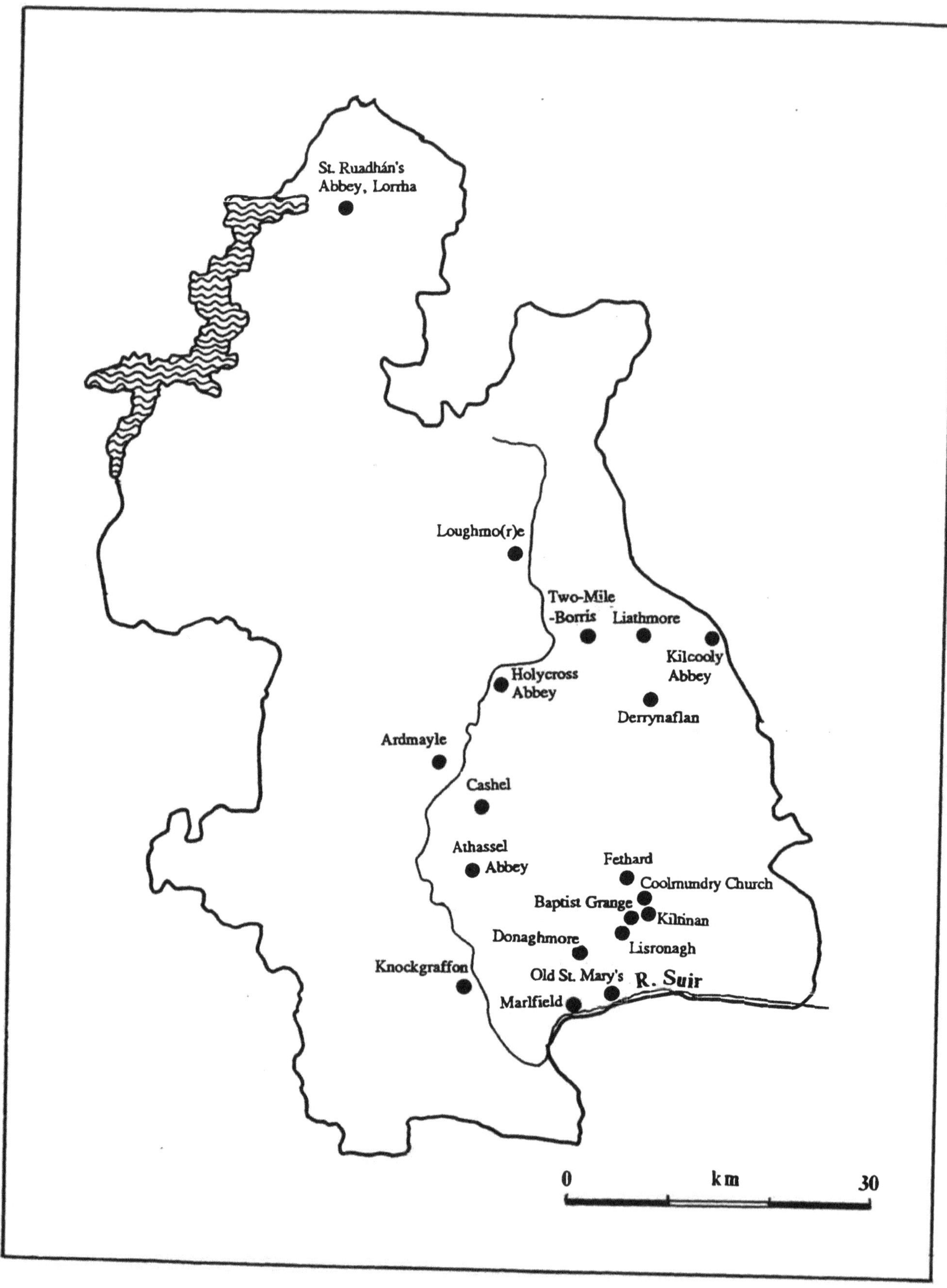

Fig. 23 Location map of sites in county Tipperary at which medieval grave-slabs occur.

CATALOGUE

INTRODUCTION

This catalogue comprises a detailed description of each of the one hundred and seven medieval grave-slabs found on twenty-two separate sites in Co. Tipperary. The descriptions are accompanied by plates. The catalogue is arranged according to the name of the site, listed in alphabetical order. Each entry contains the following information: name of site; townland; SMR number; National Grid Reference, and the classification of the slab. A brief historical and archaeological introduction to each site precedes the individual descriptions of the slabs. The descriptions give an account of the size, shape, location, condition, iconography, and inscriptions (if any) of each slab. In the case of inscriptions which are no longer decipherable, previously published transcriptions will be referred to where relevant, otherwise readings are offered. The slabs are all of limestone and in the case of slabs which survive as fragments or portions maximum measurements are used, unless otherwise stated. The principal source of reference for the historical information on each site is Gwynn, A. and Hadcock, R.N., *Medieval Religious Houses: Ireland*, (Dublin, 1970). The two main sources for the architectural descriptions of the sites are Leask, H.G., *Irish Churches and Monastic Buildings*, (Dundalk, 1955-61) and Harbison, P., *The Shell Guide to Ireland*, (Dublin, 1989). In the cases of unpublished sites new architectural summary descriptions are offered. For each individual slab the main published reference(s), if any, are given at the end of each entry.

The catalogue entries are based on fieldwork at sixty-six medieval ecclesiastical sites. Of these, only twenty-two produced grave-slabs relevant to this work. The sites inspected mainly comprise all of those medieval establishments noted in Gwynn and Hadcock (1970) and all sites where medieval or potential medieval slabs were recorded in the *Journal of the Association for the Preservation of the Memorials of the Dead* or other publications. A selection of medieval parish church sites and their graveyards, for which no relevant grave-slabs were on record, were also inspected. This selection does not represent all such sites as the Sites and Monuments Record for County Tipperary was not published at the time this fieldwork was carried out. It is expected that this catalogue will be expanded in time through further fieldwork and excavation as well as graveyard clean-up schemes.

The field methodology for this research involved, firstly, a careful search of each site for previously unrecorded slabs. This exercise resulted in an increase by approximately two-thirds of the total number of relevant slabs. Once located, each slab or fragment was examined and a written record of it, with measurements, was made. It was then photographed and a rubbing or a series of rubbings of its upper surface was made. The rubbings were made on large sheets of newsprint using wax crayon or charcoal. Later the description was amended or added to on the basis of the details evidenced in the rubbings or photographs. Each slab was subsequently revisited to check the accuracy of the written description. It was not feasible to undertake a geological assessment of the slabs, though the vast majority were clearly formed from limestone. The advice of a geologist was used, however, to assess the slabs from Athassel.

Site Name	Ardmayle Church
Townland	Ardmayle
SMR No.	T1052-034
N.G.R.	2059/14611

An early nineteenth century Church of Ireland church stands at this site, at the western end of which is attached a castellated tower. Its crenellations and turret are of the nineteenth century (An Foras Forbatha 1975) but the tower belongs to a medieval parish church (O'Flanagan 1930, 86). The modern church is a single cell of three bays and has been restored by FAS. It is situated in the centre of a large graveyard.

1. GROUP: 5
A tapered slab which originally had a pointed top, though the upper sinister corner is now broken off. It measures 1.12m in height above ground level, .53m in width near its top, .48m in width at its base, and .12m in average thickness. It stands in the graveyard, facing east, outside the east window of the church. Its decorated surface bears a slight lichen covering and the design is somewhat weathered. This is incised and consists of an interlaced seven-armed cross with trefoil terminals, enclosed within an outline circle. At the centre of this design is a quadribbed floral motif. The cross-head surmounts a plain outline shaft. There is no evidence to suggest that the slab bore an inscription.
Bibliography: Unpublished.

Site Name	Athassel Abbey
Townland	Athassel Abbey North
SMR No.	T1068-013
N.G.R.	20111/13643

This abbey, which is situated on the east bank of the river Suir, south of Golden, was built *c.* 1200

A.D. by William de Burgo and was dedicated to St. Edmund. It is the largest medieval priory in Ireland and was founded for the Canons Regular of St. Augustine. It was burned by Lord John FitzThomas in 1319 and by Brian O'Brien in 1329. John Cablis became prior there in 1394. In 1400 the priory was unlawfully detained by Robert Macmagyn and William de Burgo was recalled from a French monastery to take up the position of abbot. In the following year de Burgo complained to the Pope that he was excommunicated by the archbishop when he arrived at Athassel, and that the canons there refused to acknowledge his authority. In 1445 the priory was again unlawfully detained by Edmund Stapaton, who was later displaced by Richard de Burgo. In 1447 Geoffrey de Burgo was wounded in trying to protect the monastery from attack. David Hackett became bishop of Ossory in 1460, and in 1482 he was prior of Athassel. Between 1524-51 the priory was held in commendam by Edmund Butler, archbishop of Cashel. In 1541 it was leased to Dermot Ryan. In 1557 Athassel was granted to Thomas, Earl of Ormond and Ossory (Gwynn and Hadcock 1970, 157-8).

It was common for the Canons Regular to choose rural localities for their sites in order to enable expansion and development. Athassel is a good example of this, extending over 1.6 hectares. The church is cruciform in plan and measures *c.* 64m in internal length. The nave has two aisles and a belfry tower at its north-west corner. Each arm of the transept features two chapels. In the side walls of the chancel are groups of five lancets similar to those in St. Dominick's church, Cashel, built in 1243. The Athassel examples probably date to a decade earlier (Leask 1958, 96). At the crossing of the nave and chancel was a tower, probably contemporary with the earliest phases of the priory, but only its south arch survives. Leask suggests that after the burning of the church in 1447 this tower was rebuilt (1958, 97). In the wall dividing the nave from the chancel is a very fine doorway with an arched recess above it crowned by a hood moulding. Leask suggests that this recess probably held the rood and attendant statues until the fifteenth century, when it was blocked up for the erection of the tower (1958, 97). Enclosing a space of *c.*27.4 metres square are the claustral ranges which include a chapter house, a cellar wing, refectory, an outer parlour and the sacristy. Among the extra-claustral buildings is a vaulted gate house, with a bridge beyond it.

All the grave-slabs (except no. 11) are located in the chancel. The exception is lying against the south wall of the south chapel. The Athassel slabs were inspected by Mr Ward O'Malley, geologist, in consultation with the author who concluded that they were each of oolithic limestone. This is of interest as the limestone used for the construction of the monastery itself was not of this type.

1. GROUP: 5 Figs. 14m, 24

This consists of the upper portion of a tapered slab and measures .79m in length, .65m in width at its top, .55m in width at its base and .17m in average thickness. It stands against the east wall of the chancel to the north of the east window. Only the dexter edge is chamfered and this measures .05m wide. The sinister edge does not appear to have been originally chamfered. Although the decorated surface of the slab is somewhat weathered the incised design is easily decipherable. It consists of a very ornate eight-armed cruciform motif, with each arm featuring a trefoil at its terminal and midpoint. The inner trefoils of the horizontal and vertical arms are disposed outwardly, whereas those on the diagonal arms are disposed inwardly. At the centre of the cross is an interlocked circle, composed of four segments. The diagonal arms of the overall cruciform motif emanate from the centre of this circle, while its horizontal and vertical arms also commence within the broken circle, forming a central lozenge. On both sides of the base of the design three trefoils spring in a vegetal-like fashion. The inscription occurs in Lombardic lettering and commences at the top of the dexter side of the slab, running parallel to its chamfered edge. It is preceded by an equal-armed cross with expanded terminals. The lower half of the letters have been cut away as a result of the chamfering of this edge of the slab. It reads:

HIC JACET (F?)RATER (I/J)OH

which is probably to be interpreted as:

HIC JACET FRATER JOHANNUS/JOHES

(Here lies Brother John).

Bibliography: Unpublished.

2. GROUP: 5

A rectangular slab which measures 1.50m in length, .66m in width and .10m in average thickness. It lies in the chancel in front of the east window. The base of the slab and part of its lower sinister side are missing, and a crack runs across its upper face. The decorated surface is somewhat weathered. However, the design is decipherable and consists of an incised cross-head on a slender shaft, the base of which is missing. The cross-head features a lozenge-shaped centre from which the arms, with trefoil terminals, emanate. A pair of lobed tendril-like features extend out from the arm on the dexter side. Single such features extend from the dexter sides of the upper and lower arms. Linking the base of the cross-head with the shaft, is a circular knop. There is no evidence to suggest that the slab bore an inscription.

Bibliography: Unpublished.

3. GROUP: 3

A fragment of the lower portion of a slab, with no original edge surviving. It measures .55m in length, .30m in width and .18m in average thickness. It lies on the altar beneath the east window of the chancel. It bears a very lightly incised design, worn in places, which consists of the lower portion of an outline cross-stem terminating in a knop and three trefoils. Some of the latter are worn and

incomplete. There is no evidence to suggest that the slab bore an inscription.
Bibliography: Unpublished.

4. GROUP: 7
A fragment of a slab which measures .90m in length, .44m in width and .16m in average thickness. It is located beside no. 3. Part of two original edges, including the bottom one and the dexter one remain at right angles to one another. One edge features an undercut chamfer measuring .13m in width. There is no evidence to suggest that the slab bore an inscription or design.
Bibliography: Unpublished.

5. GROUP: 3
The lower portion of a slab which measures .42m in length, .22m in width at its top, .18m in width at its base and .12m in average thickness. It is located beside no. 3. It bears a lightly incised outline cross-stem terminating in a simple trefoil base. Although the decorated surface is somewhat weathered the design is decipherable. There is no evidence to suggest that the slab bore an inscription.
Bibliography: Unpublished.

6. GROUP: 7
The upper half of a tapered slab which measures 1.03m in length, .45m in width at its top, .30m in width at its base and .13m in average thickness. A chamfer occurs on the dexter side only, and measures 0.02m in width. A Lombardic inscription occurs on the face of the slab, which is somewhat weathered, commencing at the top of the dexter side and running parallel to its edge. It survives in fairly good condition and is preceded by an equal-armed cross with expanded terminals. It reads:

HIC JACET (F?)RA(G/T)ER THOMAS

which is probably to be interpreted as:

HIC JACET FRATER THOMAS

(Here lies Brother Thomas).

Bibliography: Unpublished.

7. GROUP: 3
The lower portion of a slab which measures .52m in length, .67m in width and .20m in average thickness. The decorated surface is somewhat weathered, though the design is easily decipherable and consists of the lower portion of a lightly incised outline cross-stem terminating in a trefoil motif. There is no evidence to suggest that the slab bore an inscription.
Bibliography: Unpublished.

8. GROUP: 5 Fig. 14n
This tapered slab measures 1.87m in length, .51m in width at its top, .35m in width at its base and .09m in average thickness. It lies in the chancel and is rather weathered and worn. It has two slight cracks on its face. All four edges are chamfered and measure .06m in width. An incised cross extends the length of the slab. The equal-armed cross-head with curved angles is enclosed by a circle which rests on the shaft. The upper angles of the cross-head feature poorly preserved, curvilinear motifs, while the lower angles feature quatrefoils. Beneath the cross-head and outside the circle is a circular knop. It is located at the top of the cross-stem, which terminates in another quatrefoil. There is no evidence to suggest that the slab bore an inscription.
Bibliography: Unpublished.

9. GROUP: 5 Figs. 14o, 25
This tapered slab measures 1.55m in length, .58m in width at its top, .46m in width at its base and .13m in average thickness. It lies in the chancel. Portion of the base is missing. The cross-head, which surmounts a plain outline shaft, is enclosed within an outline circle. It consists of an interlaced eight-armed cross with trefoiled terminals. At the centre of this design is a simple floral motif composed of eight triangular segments. There is no evidence to suggest that the slab bore an inscription.
Bibliography: Unpublished.

10. GROUP: 7
A tapered slab which measures 1.76m in length, .62m in width at its top, .52m in width at its base and .10m to .12m in average thickness. There is no evidence to suggest that the slab bore a design or inscription.
Bibliography: Unpublished.

11. GROUP: 5 Fig. 14p
A tapered slab which measures 1.71m in length, .63m in width at its top, .47m in width at its base and .15m in average thickness. The slab is covered in lichen. It is broken in two, but has been joined together by cement. It is secured against the south wall of the south chapel. The design consists of a lightly incised, four-armed outline cross which surmounts a shaft. The centre of the cross-head design features an eight-petalled rosette from which the four arms emanate. These are composed of an inner trefoil from which spring three stems. The central stems terminate in quinquefoils while the outer ones form simple trefoils. Beneath the cross-head are traces of foiled motifs on either side of the upper shaft; these have been damaged by the break in the stone. The shaft of the design terminates in a knop beneath which are three stems ending in trefoils. There is no evidence to suggest that the slab bore an inscription.
Bibliography: Unpublished.

12. GROUP: 7
A fragment of a slab which measures .40m in length, .44m in width and .20m in average thickness. Both edges of the fragment are chamfered and measure .09m in width. The slab is somewhat weathered and lies against the north wall of the chancel. There is no evidence to suggest that the slab bore an inscription or design.
Bibliography: Unpublished.

13. GROUP: 7
The lower portion of a tapered slab which measures .64m in length, .41m in width at its top, .37m in width at its base and .17m in average thickness. Both edges are chamfered and measure .08m in

width. It lies in the chancel near the south wall. There is no evidence to suggest that the slab bore an inscription or design.
Bibliography: Unpublished.

14. GROUP: 7
The lower portion of a tapered slab which measures .36m in length, .37m in width at its top, .35m in width at its base and has an average thickness of .21m. The dexter and sinister edges and the base of the fragment are chamfered and measure .10m, .06m and .07m in width respectively. It lies in the chancel near a tomb niche in the north wall. There is no evidence to suggest that the slab bore an inscription, or design.
Bibliography: Unpublished.

Site Name	Baptist Grange Church
Townland	Baptist Grange
SMR Site No.	T1077-008
N.G.R.	22124/13012

INTRODUCTION
This site is not regarded as a conventual monastery, but rather as an important grange of St. John the Baptist's, Dublin (Gwynn and Hadcock 1970, 216). Surviving is a nave and chancel church with the east and west gables still intact. There is a large gap in each of the north and south walls. The church has a dense growth of ivy and the only visible feature are the remains of an east window. The graveyard enclosed by the site's boundary wall is overgrown.

1. GROUP: 1
This consists of a portion of a tapered sandstone slab which measures 1.15m in length above ground level, .55m in width at its top, .49m in width at its base and .20m in average thickness. It stands outside the east wall of the church in an inverted, west-facing position. It is badly weathered and its decorated surface is severely worn. As a result only the cross-stem and traces of the design at the present top of the slab are decipherable. This design, which is grooved, is composed of a rectangular outline panel, within which are two vertical grooves, from which runs a double outline cross-shaft. The original top of the slab is either buried below ground level or is missing. There is no evidence to suggest that the slab bore an inscription.
Bibliography: Unpublished.

Site Name	Coolmundry Church
Townland	Strike Upper
SMR Site No.	T1070-08101
N.G.R.	22327/13291

This site consists of the ruins of a medieval church and graveyard, situated on a west-facing hill in Grove Estate. No historical information is on record for this site. The church is of nave and chancel type. Only the foundations of the chancel survive. It is smaller and narrower than the nave, which retains only part of its north and south walls. The foundation of the west wall also survives. No windows or doorways survive. The graveyard is enclosed in a subcircular area delimited by a bank, which is most obvious along the east and south, and may be an early medieval foundation.

1. GROUP: 1 Fig. 14a
This tapered, sandstone slab measures .84m in height above ground level, .46m in width at its top, .35m in width at its base and .15m in average thickness. It stands south-east of the church, in the graveyard. Its decorated surface is weathered and lichen-covered. It bears a cross, consisting of three parallel grooves forming the cross-stem, emanating from a subcircular cross-head with the remains of three short, projecting arms. The sinister side of the cross head does not survive. A grooved border runs around both sides and across the top of the face of the slab, and measures .03m in width. There is no evidence to suggest that the slab bore an inscription.
Bibliography: Unpublished.

Site Name	Derrynaflan Church
Townland	Lurgoe
SMR Site No.	T1054-00204
N.G.R.	21807/14957

This thirteenth century church stands on an island in a bog on the site of a monastery founded by St. Ruadhán of Lorrha in the sixth century. It is referred to locally as "the Island" or "the Goban Saor". The latter appelation derives from the local belief that the burial-place of this well-known mythological character occurs in the small trapezoidal enclosure to the south-east of the church (O'Donovan 1840, 523-534; O hOgain 1935, 264-5 and *anon.* 1833, 112). The remains of the church consist of the east, south and north walls of the chancel. The nave is represented only by the foundations of its south wall. The east wall of the chancel features two single-light, trefoiled-headed, chamfered windows which splay inwards. The lower portion of a window survives in the north wall. A round-headed piscina is set into the south wall in a secondary position. The chancel was added to the nave sometime in the thirteenth century. The west wall of a building of uncertain purpose remains to the north of the church (Leask 1958, 147; Harbison 1970, 227). A series of excavations have been carried out by the National Museum at this site during the 1980s (Ryan 1983).

The medieval slabs lie in a modern enclosed area north-east of the thirteenth-century church.

1. GROUP: 2 Figs. 8, 14e
This consists of a tapered slab in two portions. The upper portion measures 1.60m in length, .41m in width at its top, .33m in width at its base and .21m in average thickness. The lower fragment measures .42m in length, .31m in width at its top, .29m in

width at its base and .21m in average thickness. The upper surface of the slab is weathered and chipped and parts of its long edges are broken. A head is carved in high relief at the top of its upper surface. Portion of this head is defaced, and its only surviving features are the base of the nose, the mouth and the neck. At the base of the slab what appear to be stylised feet are carved in high relief. The rest of the design is incised and extends the length of the slab. A circle occurs beneath the head and encloses a cross formed from the juxtapositioning of four penannular circles. At the centre of the cross is thus formed a lozenge and this motif is repeated at the end of the arms. It may also have occurred at the terminals of the cross-shaft, but it does not survive here. Two single stems with lobed terminals extend upwards from the enclosing circle. Between the dexter stem and the carved-head is a circular design formed from four lentoids disposed around a small circle. Linked to the enclosing circle by a pair of grooves is a small human head which features eyes, a nose and a mouth. A double outline central shaft extends from the base of the small human head to the carved 'feet' at the base of the slab. Two smaller stems extend out, upwardly disposed from this central shaft ending in lobed terminals. Two similar stems extend out from its base. There is no evidence to suggest that the slab bore an inscription.
Bibliography: Maher, D., 1994, 162-66

2. GROUP: 2
A tapered slab surviving in four portions which are reset in concrete. The reset slab measures 1.10m in length, .33m in width at its top, .20m in width at its base and .10m in average thickness. It survives in a rather weathered condition. The only apparent design is an extremely defaced head, carved in relief at the top of the slab. There is no evidence to suggest that the slab bore an inscription.
Bibliography: *ibid,* 162-3

3. GROUP: 2
This consists of two portions of a tapered slab. The upper portion measures .5m in length, .8m in maximum surviving width and .09m in average thickness. The lower portion measures 1.14m in length, .75m in width at its top, .65m in width at its base and .11m in average thickness. Its decorated surface is weathered. The upper portion features two defaced human heads in relief. The mouth and neck are the only surviving features of the head on the dexter side. No features survive on the other head. A motif in relief, consisting of four lentoids in a circle, occurs between the two carved heads. Beneath the two carved heads are the remains of two poorly preserved incised crosses contained within outline circles which surmount narrow, partly surviving, cross-stems. The crosses are each formed from a juxtapositioning of four penannular circles, which results in a cross with expanded terminals and hollowed angles. The sinister example features an incised circle at its centre.
Bibliography: *ibid,* 163

Site Name	Donaghmore Church
Townland	Donaghmore
SMR Site No.	T1077-02701
N.G.R.	21877/12906

Little is on record concerning the history of this church, except that it was founded by St. Farranan. He died in 982 at Waser on the Meuse, after voluntary exile on the Continent (Harbison 1970, 226). The church is a good example of a Romanesque building of moderate size. It consists of a nave and chancel. The west doorway is finely ornamented although most of its decoration is poorly preserved. The carving survives best on the voussoirs and piers of the second order. The hood-mould is said to have formerly contained a tympanum on which was carved a cat with two tails (probably a lion). The other interesting feature at this church is the chancel-arch, of three orders, of which only the piers remain. The chancel is smaller and narrower than the nave. The high-pitched gables of the church which are almost complete, also survive. A plain vault covers the chancel and above this is a croft, which is lighted by a small window in the east wall. It is entered by a doorway over the chancel arch. There are two small round-headed windows in the south wall of the church which light the nave. There is another such window near the centre of the north wall. Close to the east corner of the north wall is a later window. All the windows splay inwards. Portions of the upper and south walls were restored in the sixteenth century (Crawford 1909, 261-4; Leask 1955, 136-7).

Slab no. 1 lies in the chancel, while slab no. 2 stands east of the church in the graveyard.

1. GROUP: 5 Figs. 14g, 26
This slab survives in three somewhat weathered portions. The upper portion measures .79m in length, .46m in width and .10m in average thickness; the middle portion measures .38m in length, .34m in width and .08m in average thickness, and the lower portion measures .45m in length, .41m in width and .08m in average thickness. The three portions fit together but a large piece of the slab's sinister side is missing. All the surviving edges of the remaining portions are chamfered and measure .02m in width. The slab bears a cross in relief and features a raised border, .08m in width, along its dexter and sinister sides and along its top. The arms of the cross-head terminate in simple trefoils with single cross-bands separating these from the arms. A pair of such bands divides the cross-head from the shaft and another, single, example occurs at the base of the shaft surmounting a pillar-base form. There is no evidence to suggest that the slab bore an inscription.
Bibliography: Unpublished.

2. GROUP: 5 Figs. 14c, 27
This slightly tapered sandstone slab measures 1m in length, .44m in width at its top, .42m in width at its base and .12m in average thickness. Both the sinister and dexter edges are chamfered and

measure .09m in width. The slab is set upright in concrete. Although it has been subjected to weathering, its design, in relief, is decipherable. The upper portion consists of a sunken circular area in which an equal-armed cross with bifid terminals occurs in relief; a lozenge-shaped sunken area occurs at the centre of the cross. The enclosing circle of the cross rests on a broad outlined shaft, on either side of which is a broad, shallowly rectilinear panel with bifid top. There is no evidence to suggest that the slab bore an inscription.
Bibliography: Unpublished.

Site Name	Fethard Augustinian Friary
Townland	Fethard
SMR Site No.	T1070-040
N.G.R.	22078/13497

This friary was founded around 1306 by the Order of Hermits of St. Augustine (the Augustinian Friars). Walter de Mulcote introduced the friars to Fethard and granted them one and half acres of land which he held free of all service from Maurice Mac Carwall, the Archbishop of Cashel. A commission held at Cashel in 1306 found that de Mulcotes grant had been made contrary to mortmain and without the permission of King Edward I. Within a few months Edward had issued a writ pardoning the friars at Fethard for acquiring the land. The holdings of the friars were increased with the receipt of two royal grants. By the early sixteenth century Fethard was one of the richest mendicant friaries in Ireland. In 1554, however, the monastery was granted, with its lands, to the Baron of Dunboyne (Edmund Butler). The Augustinians regained possession of the ruins of the monastery in the early nineteenth century (Gwynn and Hadcock 1970, 299-300).

In 1820 the church was renovated resulting in its re-roofing and the demolition of the massive square tower which stood at its entrance. A small belfry and facade of cut stone replaced the tower. The altar and sanctuary were also remodelled. The medieval features surviving at the site include the church, the east cloister range, the ruins of a transept chapel which lies to the north of the church and a two-storyed building adjacent to the south side of the chancel, the lower storey of which is a chapel. Inside the church there are three fifteenth century arches which feature an interesting collection of mason's marks (Maher 1992). All except four of the windows are nineteenth century additions: two occur immediately east of the transeptal chapel and date to the fourteenth century, as does the window high up in the north wall overlooking the main altar; beneath the latter window, nearer to ground level, is a fifteenth century window.

The surviving *ex situ* architectural fragments include a stone-carved figure which has been interpreted as a Sheela-na-gig (on an outside wall running east of the church), a small fourteenth century human head and a late medieval tomb cover, both built into the north wall of the sacristy. Also surviving is a large fourteenth century head - capital flanked by foliage motifs, located on top of the east-west flanking wall south of the church (O'Keefe 1995).

The medieval grave-slabs are located in and around the ruins of the north transept chapel.

1. GROUP: 4 Fig. 14q
A rectangular slab which measures 1.62m in length, .78m in width and .12m in average thickness. It is the most easterly of the group of slabs which lie against the outer face of the north wall of the north transept chapel. While the top corners of the slab are chipped it survives in good condition overall. The design consists of a seven-armed segmental cross, carved in relief, with each arm terminating in a fleur-de-lis. Three simple cross-bands occur at the base of the cross-head, surmounting the cross-shaft. A similar design occurs at the base of the shaft, but survives poorly. The cross terminates in what appears to be a stylised pillar-base feature. An inscription in Black Letter occurs on the dexter and sinister sides and across the top of the slab. It survives in poor condition and is illegible except for the following on its dexter side:

....MARGARETA....TUMULI FIERI FECERU/"
(....Margaret who caused this tomb to be made).

Bibliography: Unpublished.

2. GROUP: 4
A rectangular slab which stands 1.58m in height above ground level and measures 1.13m in width. Both of the long edges feature a chamfer and an undercut chamfer which measure .04m and .11m in width respectively. It stands against the outer face of the north wall of the ruins of the north transept chapel, and a good deal of its lower portion is buried beneath ground level. It survives in good condition, although the decorated surface is somewhat weathered. The design consists of a seven-armed segmental cross, carved in relief, with fleur-de-lis terminals. Each of the four segments at the centre of the cross-head feature a foliate design. At the base of the cross-head four cross-bands occur, surmounting the cross-shaft. The base of the latter is not visible. Two worn heraldic shields occur on either side of the shaft. That on the sinister side features a plain chief, beneath which are two quadrupeds rampant with antlers or prominent ears on either side of a shield of pretence. The dexter shield is divided into a number of sections: the first one-third of the chief on its dexter end is indented, with two dice-like charges below it, and similar indentations occur on the fesse point. Portion of an inscription in Black Letter survives along the sinister side of the slab. It survives as:

HIC JACET THEOBALDUS BUTLER DE DARRELUSKAN GENEROSUS ET.....

This has been translated by Knowles (1903, 142) as follows:

Here lies Theobald Butler of Darreloskan, Gentleman, and Catherine.

Bibliography: Knowles, J.A., 1903, 142.

3. GROUP: 4
The lower portion of a rectangular slab which measures 1.11m in height above ground level, .93m in width and .11m in average thickness. Both the sinister and dexter edges bear a chamfer measuring .03m in width. The slab stands against the outer face of the north wall of Our Lady's chapel. Its decorated surface is somewhat weathered. The design, which is in relief, consists of the lower portion of a cross-shaft which terminates in a pillar-base form. On either side of it are two worn heraldic shields, the dexter example featuring a decorative base. An inscription in Black Letter occurs along the dexter and sinister edges of the slab. It is very worn and only the following is legible:

Sinister" *1A...2O (N?)US UXORE....F.ERIB9/.*
Dexter: *....MAII....*

Bibliography: Unpublished.

4. GROUP: 5 Fig. 14h
A rectangular slab which stands 1.50m in height above ground level, and measures .96m in width and .19m in average thickness. It stands against the outer face of the north wall of Our Lady's chapel and survives in good condition. The decorated surface bears a broad border and bears a cross in relief. The transverse terminals of the cross end in trefoils while the upper terminal merges with the border. Three cross-bands occur at the base of the cross-head, surmounting the cross-shaft. A similar motif occurs at the base of the shaft, surmounting a pillar-base form. The *sol et lunulae* motif occurs at the top of the slab: the former occupying the dexter corner and the latter the sinister corner. The sinister edge of the slab features roll-mouldings, and there is no evidence to suggest that the slab bore an inscription.

Bibliography: Unpublished.

5. GROUP: 5 Fig. 14i
This rectangular slab measures 1.74m in height above ground level, .83m in width and .12m in average thickness. The sinister edge and top of the slab feature multiple mouldings which is broken along the top of the slab. It stands against the outer face of the north wall of the north transept chapel and survives in good condition. Its design consists of a cross in relief, with a large trefoil at each arm terminal. These arms emanate from a lozenge-shaped centre. Three cross-bands occur at the base of the cross-head, surmounting the cross-shaft. A similar feature occurs at the base of the shaft surmounting the cross-base, portion of which is buried. A narrow raised border occurs along the margin of the design of the cross, and the slab features a broad border An inscription in Roman lettering commences along the sinister side of the slab and continues along the shaft and head of the cross. It has been published by Knowles (1903, 145) as follows:

HI QUAMVIS TUMULO SAXOQUE PREMENTE QUIESCANT TU TAMEN HIS REQUIEM QUAM PETIERE VOVE. BEATI. MORTUI QU. IN. DOMINO. MORIUNTUR.

Knowles (1903, 145) translated the Latin verse as follows:

(Although beneath this tomb in ashes now they lie still grant them thou O Lord! The rest they craved on high.).

The following groups of letters occur on the cross-head:

M.M.M.M. S.U.A.M. N.S.M.S. M.M.D. O.M.D.M.M.

The meaning of these is uncertain.

Bibliography: Knowles, J.A., 1903, 145.

6. GROUP: 4
This rectangular slab measures 1.33m in height above ground level, .86m in width and .11m in average thickness. A substantial amount of its base is buried. The sinister edge features a chamfer and an undercut chamfer, measuring .03m in width and .12m in width respectively. It stands against the outer face of the east wall of the north transept chapel. Its decorated surface is somewhat worn and features a broad border along both sides. The design consists of a seven-armed segmental cross in relief with fleur-de-lis terminals. Two simple cross-bands occur at the base of the cross-head, surmounting the cross-shaft. An inscription in Black Letter commences on the dexter border and continues between it and the cross-shaft. It is very worn and only the date is legible:

MCCCC(C)VIII
(1508?).

Bibliography: Unpublished.

7. GROUP: 4
A rectangular slab which measures 2.17m in length, at least .59m in width and .14m in average thickness. It is one of three *ex situ* slabs which together form a tomb located beneath the arch in the east wall of the north transept chapel; the second slab is no. 8 in this catalogue, while the third is of mid-seventeenth century date. This slab forms the east side of the tomb, and stands on its dexter edge. Its decorated surface is somewhat weathered. The top corner on the sinister side is broken and the dexter edge is not visible due to the positioning of the slab. The design consists of a seven-armed segmental cross carved in relief. Three cross-bands occur at the base of the cross-head, surmounting the cross-shaft. A similar feature occurs at the base of the shaft, surmounting a pillar-base form. The inscription, which is in Black Letter is visible only on the sinister side and across the base of the slab. It reads:

HIC JACET TOMAS FILIUS O.... LE BUT(T)LET E(T) (J?)OH?(A)N(NA) (F)ILIA DERM(OT) ...

This was translated by Knowles (1903, 110) as:

(Here lies Thomas, son of Edmund le Buttler and Johanna, daughter of Dermot O'Mulryan, A.D. 1524).

Bibliography: Knowles, J.A., 1903, 110.

8 GROUP: 4
A rectangular slab which measures 2.06m in length, .62m in width and .16m in average thickness. All four edges are chamfered and measure .05m in width. It forms the top of a tomb made up of three such slabs and survives in good condition. The design consists of a seven-armed segmental fleur-de-lis cross, carved in relief. Three cross-bands occur at the base of the cross-head, surmounting the cross-shaft. A single such band occurs at the base of the shaft, surmounting a pillar-base form. There is no evidence to suggest that the slab bore an inscription.
Bibliography: Unpublished.

9. GROUP: 4 Fig. 28
A rectangular slab which measures 2.08m in length, and 1.02m in width. All four edges bear a chamfer measuring .02m in width. It is set against the inner face of the east wall of the north transept chapel, in an upright position. It survives in good condition, but there is one crack which runs diagonally across the upper sinister side. The design consists of a seven-armed segmental cross, carved in relief, with fleur-de-lis terminals. Four cross-bands occur at the base of the cross-head, surmounting the cross-shaft. Three such cross-bands occur at the base of the shaft, surmounting a pillar-base form. A raised border runs around the slab and features an inscription in Black Letter on both the dexter and sinister sides. Brennan (1863, 246) transcribed the inscription as follows:

HIC JACENT THADEUS O' MEAGHER DE BALLIDIN & ANASTATIA PURTIA ETI'/UXOR QUI ME FIERI FECERUT 20 MAII./ANNO SALUTIS 1600.

This latter transcription is inaccurate and should read:

HIC IACET THADAEUS DONILL O MEAGHER DE BALIDINI ET ANASTATIA PUR(R?)TIA/ETI' UXOR QUI ME FIERI FECERUT 20 MAII A DNI 1600.

It was translated by Knowles (1903, 115) as:

(Here lies Thadeus Donall O, Meagher of Ballidiul and Anastatia Purcell his wife, who caused this monument to be erected, the 20th day of May, A.D. 1600).

Bibliography: Brennan, 1863, 246; Knowles, J.A., 1903, 115.

10. GROUP: 4
This rectangular slab measures 1.90m in length, .68m in width and .12m in average thickness. It lies on its sinister side, inside the east wall of the north transept chapel. A large portion of the dexter side is broken off. The design consists of a seven-armed segmental cross carved in relief, with fleur-de-lis terminals. Three cross-bands occur at the base of the cross-head, surmounting the cross-shaft. A similar feature occurs at the base of the shaft, surmounting a pillar-base form. The three arms on the dexter side are missing due to the break. An inscription in Roman lettering commences at the base, and continues along the dexter side and across the top of the slab. The surviving inscription reads:

PROSE. SUAQUE/PROGENIE. 24..../ REDMU.....

Knowles (1903, 125) translated the full inscription as:

Redmund Vinn, who caused this stone to be erected to the memory of himself and his children, 24 December .....

Bibliography: Knowles, J.A., 1903, 125.

11. GROUP: 4 Fig. 29
A long rectangular slab which measures 2.17m in length, .98m in width and .07m in average thickness. The sinister, top and basal edges bear a chamfer which measures .03m in width. The slab lies on its dexter side between the junction of the east wall of the ruined chapel and the north wall of the main church. Its lower sinister corner is broken. The design consists of a seven-armed, segmental, fleur-de-lis cross, carved in relief. Foliate and other indecipherable forms occur in the four sunken segments of the cross-head. At its base three cross-bands occur, separated by two narrow bands of diagonal lines. This feature surmounts the cross-shaft which terminates in three simple cross-bands which surmount the base of the cross; the latter is of elaborate pillar-base form. On the dexter side of the cross-shaft the letters IHC (IHS) occur in Black Letter. A heraldic shield occurs on the opposite side of the shaft and features an indented chief, charged with a bend. An inscription in Black Letter occurs on the top, base and along the sinister side of the slab. Only the inscription along the top is now legible. This portion reads:

HIC JACET THADEUS OWNS MEAGHER....
(Here lies Thadeus Owns Meagher....).

Knowles (1903, 113) published its full translation as follows:

Here lie Thaddeus Owns Meagher and Honora Keeghan, his wife, who erected this monument before their death, A.D. 1540.

Bibliography: Knowles, J.A., 1903, 113-4.

12. GROUP: 4
This rectangular slab measures 1.75m in length, 1.06m in width and .10m in average thickness. It lies against the north wall of the church, outside the east wall of the transept chapel. The lower portion of the slab no longer survives, and one crack occurs across the centre of the upper portion. The design consists of a seven-armed segmental cross carved in relief with fleur-de-lis terminals. Three simple cross-bands occur at the base of the cross-head, surmounting the cross-shaft. A similar motif occurs at the base of the shaft. An inscription in Black Letter commences across the top of the slab and continues along the dexter side. It reads:

HIC JACET PETRUS BU(TLER)/.... .... QUI ME FIERI FECIT POIT .ORTE EI' PETRUS.....

Knowles (1903, 141) translated it as:

Here lie Peter Butler and Norah O'Quin (Or Kenny), who erected this monument. Peter Butler died XI day of Jan. A.D. 1571.

Bibliography: Knowles, J.A., 1903, 141.

13. GROUP: 4 Fig. 30
The upper portion of a rectangular slab which measures .66m in length and .66m in maximum width. Its thickness is unattainable as it is set, upside down, in the east wall of the east range. The surviving design consists of three complete arms of a seven-armed segmental cross-head. It survives in a rather worn condition, especially at the upper sinister corner where part of a Black Letter inscription survives. It is illegible.
Bibliography: Unpublished

14. GROUP: 4
A cross-head fragment which measures .26m x .10m. It is set in the south side of the north wall of the north transept chapel. It was probably part of a rectangular slab which featured a seven-armed segmental cross as its principal design. No inscription survives.
Bibliography: Unpublished.

Site Name	Fethard Holy Trinity Church
Townland	Fethard
SMR Site No.	T1070-040
N.G.R.	22078/13497

Still in use, this church, in the possession of the Church of Ireland, originated as the parish church of medieval Fethard. It was granted to St. John the Baptists, Dublin. It was probably the earliest building of the medieval town and was probably built around the early thirteenth century. The structure that survives today appears to date to the thirteenth, fifteenth and sixteenth centuries.

It consists of a large nave and chancel church, with the original chancel surviving in ruins. A small chapel and a sacristy adjoin the south walls of the nave and chancel. The remains of a sixteenth century aisle occurs outside the church on the south side. Access from this aisle to the interior of the church was by means of two arches which are now blocked up. A segment of an arch, terminating in a stone carved head, marks a doorway in the south wall of the church. The west end of the church features a substantial tower with well preserved battlements. The five-light window in the west wall of the tower is of fifteenth century date, finely decorated with floral tracery. Outside the east wall of the church is the remains of the chancel. The medieval town wall, which is situated very close to the church, occurs on its south side. Decoration in the interior of the church is minimal and the walls are now white-washed. A number of seventeenth century grave-slabs act as floor paving along the central and two side - aisles. A tomb dating to 1508, commemorating Anne Rochel and Edward Hackett, is situated behind the organ, near the north wall of the chancel.

Three of the medieval slabs of relevance are located inside the church and two are outside.

1. GROUP: 4 Fig. 32
A rectangular slab which measures 1.91m in length, .69m in width and .18m in average thickness. All four edges are chamfered and measure .03m in width. The slab lies on the ground in the porch of the church, inside the west door. The decorated surface of the slab is somewhat weathered, but both the inscription and design are easily decipherable. The design consists of a seven-armed segmental cross, carved in relief, with fleur-de-lis terminals. Two cross-bands occur at the base of the cross-head, surmounting the cross-shaft. A similar feature occurs at the base of the shaft, which terminates in a pillar-base form. An inscription in Black Letter occurs on the dexter and sinister sides and across the base and the top of the slab. It has been translated by O'Leary (1928, 162) as:

HIC JACET AEDMUNDUS FILIUS JOHANNIS EVERARD QUI OBIIT SEXTO DIE MENSIS MARTII A DO M.CCCCC. OCTAVO. CUI' AIE MICEATUR DEUS. AMEN.
(Here lies Edmund, son of John Everard, who died on the sixth day of the month of March, A.D., M.CCCCC. eight; on whose soul may God have mercy. Amen.).

Bibliography: O'Leary, E., 1928, 161-2.

2. GROUP: 3 Fig. 31
The lower portion of a tapered slab which measures .43m in length, .37m in width at its top, .41m in width at its base and .15m in average thickness. It stands inverted in the graveyard south-west of the church. Its decorated surface is somewhat weathered. The design, which is incised, consists of an outline cross-stem terminating in an outline trefoil. There is no evidence to suggest that the slab bore an inscription.
Bibliography: Unpublished.

3. GROUP: 3(?) Fig. 33
A tapered slab which measures 1.06m in length, .40m in max. width and .26m in min. width. Its thickness is unattainable as it occurs as a floor-slab in the south aisle of the church. The outline incised design consists of an encircled cross-head which features three partially surviving pennanular, interlocking circles. The remainder of the design is rather worn. A simple outline trefoil occurs at the base of the cross-stem. The outer edges of the slab are defined by a groove. There is no evidence for an original inscription, however a modern one, incised in Roman capitals, occurs across the base of the cross-head. It reads:

MEARY CONNELL

Bibliography: Unpublished

4. GROUP: 3(?)
A portion of a tapered slab which measures .75m in max. surviving length, .47m in max. width, .41m in min. width and .45m in thickness. The visible edge is chamfered. The slab, which survives in a rather worn condition, is located in a niche in the east end of the north aisle. It occurs in a secondary position, east of the Hackett and Rochel mensa. The design consists of an incised cross-stem which terminates in a stepped base. An incised lozenge, which is

quartered, occurs on the middle of the cross-stem. It is, perhaps, contemporary. An inscription in Lombardic lettering occurs along the base and sinister side. It is illegible.
Bibliography: Unpublished

5. GROUP: 3(?)
A portion of a tapered slab which measures .87m in length, .36m in minimum width, and .27m in max. width. Its thickness is unattainable as it occurs as a quoin at the south-east external angle of the nave. The design, which survives in a rather worn condition, consists of an incised cross-stem, terminating in a stepped base. There is no evidence to suggest that the slab bore an inscription.
Bibliography: Unpublished.

Site Name	Holycross Abbey
Townland	Holycross
SMR Site No.	T1047-03001
N.G.R.	20898/15420

The abbey is believed to have been a Benedictine house before its foundation by Donal Mór O'Brien in 1180, who was responsible for the arrival of the Cistercians there from Monasteranenagh, Co. Limerick. In 1227 the abbey was struggling because of bad management. In 1228 Stephen of Lexington visited Holy Cross and sent a monk there from Dunbrody to help in its administration. Following the Monasteranenagh riot the abbey was affiliated to Margam in Wales. Henry III confirmed John's Charter in 1233, taking the abbey under his protection. In 1267 Isaac Ó Cormacain became a monk at Holy Cross after he resigned the bishopric of Killaloe. In 1278 the affiliation with Monasteranenagh was restored, but was made subject to Mellifont in 1289. There were various appointments *c.* 1424 which caused internal trouble. The churches of Ballycahill, Rathkennan and Glenkeen were appropriated to the abbey in 1429, 1452 and 1486. In 1448 Abbot Odo O'Grady resigned and Dermit O'Heffernan, a monk from Rome, replaced him as abbot. Dermit was replaced by Matthew Omubceayn, a monk of Abington in 1445. The abbey was changed into a provostship with the general suppression, and Abbot Philip Purcell was appointed provost. In 1563 the abbey, along with over 420 acres, was granted to the Ormonds. The monks remained there and Bernard Foley became abbot in 1602. In 1618 Holy Cross was the general novitiate for the Irish Cistercians under abbot Luke Archer. The last monk died in 1752 (Gwynn and Hadcock 1970, 134-5).

Holy Cross abbey - well known for its association with a fragment of the True Cross - features an eastern arm, a transept, a crossing tower, a cloister arcade and the east and west ranges of domestic buildings. It also features a necessarium, an infirmary and the abbots' lodging. Because of meagre documentary evidence exact dating for the various buildings is lacking. However, some clues may be got from the structure itself. It is assumed that the building of the eastern arm of the church dates to the third quarter of the fifteenth century, based on a Black Letter inscription carved in relief on either side of a shield situated on the south-east pier of the cloister arcade (Leask 1960, 60). Leask also concludes that the most active period in the "native style" dates to between 1450 and 1475 (1960, 60). Only the plain thirteenth century nave of the original church survives, and a doorway leading from the south aisle to the cloister is probably late twelfth century in date. The 'later' church displays attractive architecture, featuring a broad tower, a transept with two chapels in each arm and a nave with aisles. In the west wall traces of the original lancet windows are to be seen. The doorway to the cloister walk is round-arched and is executed in sandstone. The windows display great variety in design, with the east window being the largest. It consists of six lights, ogee-headed and cusped, beneath uncusped tracery. The west doorway is small with a segmental arch on the inside and a pointed one on the outside. Another interesting feature is the sedilia, situated in the south wall of the chancel, known better as "the tomb of the Good Woman's son". It is one of the better works of its kind and bears the arms of the Earls of Ormond and the English royal arms. The west wall of the north transept preserves one of the few medieval wall paintings surviving in Ireland. It depicts a hunting scene, coloured in brown, red and green. There are two features of interest in the south transept: the 'monks' waking place' - a tomb-like box structure - which may have been used to house the relic of the True Cross, and the night stairs leading to the first floor of the domestic buildings. Of the claustral buildings only the west and dorter ranges remain, having been rebuilt in the fifteenth century. Only the foundations of the south range survives. There are further structures east of the claustral ranges, probably an infirmary and abbots' quarters (Leask 1960, 60-69.

The grave-slabs are located in the cloister and in the chancel and north and south chapel of the church.

1. GROUP: 4
A tapered slab in two portions: the upper portion measures 1.51m in length, .48m in width at its top, .44m in width at its base and .15m in average thickness; the lower portion measures .51m in length, .44m in width at its top, .43m in width at its base and .15m in average thickness. The slab lies inside the south wall of the cloister. Its decorated surface is worn and is heavily lichen - covered. The upper dexter portion of the slab is broken. The design consists of a seven-armed segmental cross, carved in relief, with simple fleur-de-lis terminals. Three narrow cross-bands occur at the base of the cross-head, surmounting the cross-shaft. The remainder of the design occurs on the lower portion and consists of the lower end of the cross-shaft terminating in a pillar-base form. All four edges of the slab are rounded. There is no evidence to suggest that the slab bore an inscription.
Bibliography: Unpublished.

2. GROUP: 7
The upper portion of a tapered slab which measures 1.09m in length, .53m in width at its top, .47m in width at its base and .15m in average thickness. It lies at the south end of the cloister. It survives in a worn condition, the base is missing and the edges are chipped. There is no evidence to suggest that the slab bore an inscription or design.
Bibliography: Unpublished.

3. GROUP: 7
The upper portion of a tapered slab which measures .94m in length, .48m in width at its top, .44m in width at its base and .17m in average thickness. It lies among other slabs at the south end of the cloister. Its upper surface is chipped and worn. There is no evidence to suggest that it bore an inscription or design.
Bibliography: Unpublished.

4. GROUP: 7
The upper portion of a tapered slab which measures 1.28m in length, .54m in width at its top and .12m in average thickness. Its width at the base is unattainable due to its position beneath no. 3. Both the dexter and sinister edges are chamfered, measuring .08m in width. It lies among other slabs at the south end of the cloister. The slab is worn and the base is missing. There is no evidence to suggest that it bore an inscription or design.
Bibliography: Unpublished.

5. GROUP: 3
The lower portion of a tapered slab which measures .61m in length, .3m in width at its top, .27m in width at its base. The dexter, sinister and basal edges are chamfered, measuring .08m in width. It lies among other slabs at the south end of the cloister. Its decorated surface is worn and lichen covered. One crack occurs parallel to the cross-shaft. The design consists of an outline cross-shaft which terminates in a trefoil base. There is no evidence to suggest that it bore an inscription.
Bibliography: Unpublished.

6. GROUP: 4
A tapered slab in two portions which measures 1.84m in length, .5m in width at its top, .4m in width at its base and .12m in average thickness. All of its four edges are chamfered and measure .04m in width. It lies among other slabs at the south end of the cloister. Its decorated surface is worn and the design consists of an eight-armed fleur-de-lis cross, carved in relief, terminating in a stepped base. The middle foil of the lower vertical arm joins up with the shaft, and a knop occurs further down the shaft carved in low relief. There is no evidence to suggest that the slab bore an inscription.
Bibliography: Unpublished.

7. GROUP: 4 Fig. 14c
This tapered slab measures 1.97m in length, .65m in width at its top and .52m in width at its base. Its thickness is unattainable. It lies in the chancel behind the altar. The slab has obviously been polished to a marble-like finish. It survives in good condition, except for two cracks. The design consists of a seven-armed segmental cross, with each arm terminating in a fleur-de-lis. Three cross-bands occur at the base of the cross-head, surmounting the cross-shaft. One single cross-band occurs at the base of the cross-shaft surmounting a pillar-base form. A pair of interlocked rectangular forms, open at the base and framed by a broad border, occupy the centre of the slab. An inscription in Black Letter occurs on all four sides and along the cross-shaft. It has been published by Fitzgerald (1901, 104) as follows:

HIC JACET NOBILIS/AC GENEROSUS VIR JACOBUS PURSELL BARO DE CORKHYNY ET LIBOLBY ET BALLYCORMMYC AC DNS DE/ CHRIPURSELLYE Q OBIIT II°/DIE MENSIS MAII A:D:[illegible word] *MCCCCCV ET ... A BUTLER UXOR EIUS.*

This inscription has been translated by Hayes (1970, 16) as follows:

(Here lies the noble and highborn man James Purcell, Baron of Corkatenny, Lisbothy and Ballymormuck, and Lord of Chripurselluc who died on the second of May, A.D. 1505. Also Ellen Butler his wife).

The inscription along the shaft is too worn to decipher.
Bibliography: Fitzgerald, W., 1901, 104; Hayes, W.J., 1970, 16.

8. GROUP: 4
This tapered slab measures 1.93m in length, .65m in width at its top and .61m in width at its base. Its thickness is unattainable, as it acts as a floor slab in the chancel behind the altar. It survives in good condition, however, its decorated surface is somewhat worn. The design consists of a seven-armed cross with fleur-de-lis terminals. A knop occurs at the base of the cross-head, surmounting the cross-shaft, and a similar feature occurs at the base of the shaft surmounting a pillar-base form. An inscription in Black Letter occurs on the dexter and sinister sides and across the base. It is very worn and is largely illegible, but the christian name and the date are decipherable:

HIC JACET JACOBUS BU(T?)(L?)ER..../ 159(7?).

(Here Lies Jacob Butler .... 1597?).
Bibliography: Unpublished.

9. GROUP: 4 Fig. 34
A slightly tapered slab which measures 2.17m in length, .73m in width at its top, .67m in width at its base. A chamfer occurs along the dexter and sinister edges and along the base, it measures .03m in width. There is also an undercut chamfer, which is visible only on the dexter side, measuring .16m in width. The slab is set in a tomb niche in the north wall of the chancel which is preserved as a semi-circular headed-niche of carved limestone with a projecting hood-mould. Built into the front of the niche is an end-slab of a tomb chest which is carved in false relief and features The Crucifixion under an ogee-headed niche. Our Lady occupies the dexter side, also under an ogee-headed niche.

This inserted end-slab has been dated to the mid-sixteenth century (Hunt 1974, cat. 240).

The decorated surface of the tomb-lid is chipped and worn. The design, which is in relief, consists of a seven-armed segmental cross, with simple fleurs-de-lis terminals to each arm. Three cross-bands occur at the base of the cross-head surmounting the cross-shaft, and three similar cross-bands occur at the base of the cross-shaft above a pillar-base form. An inscription in Black Letter occurs along the dexter and sinister sides of the slab, across its base and along the shaft and base of the cross. It has been published by Fitzgerald (1901, 103) as follows:

HIC IACENT DISCRETI HOMES S. DONATUS O'FOGARTA ET ELINA PORSELL UXOR EIUS QU OBYT. A. DO.IMCCCCC.

It has been translated by Hayes (1970, 18) as follows:

(Here lie the worthy persons, Donagh O'Fogarty and Helen Pursell, his wife. He died in the year 15..).

On the opposite side:

SALUTA ME DE MARIE P.... DE DONAT ET E'. QUORUM AIA.

This consists of an unfinished sentence and is probably a request by the deceased for prayers for his soul.

Bibliography: Fitzgerald, W., 1901, 103; Hunt, J., 1974, cat. 240; Hayes, W.J., 1970, 17-8.

10. GROUP: 3 Fig. 14j

This slightly tapered slab measures 1.43m in length, .59m in width at its top, .58m in width at its base. The sinister edge is chamfered and measures .04m in width. The dexter edge of the slab abuts against the north wall of the most northerly chapel in the north transept. The slab survives in fairly good condition but its decorated surface is somewhat worn and its base is broken off. The design consists of an incised outline cross, with a trefoil at the terminal of each arm. The trefoils of the upper and the sinister arms only partially survive, as does the outline cross-shaft. There is no evidence to suggest that the slab bore an inscription.

Bibliography: Unpublished.

11. GROUP: 4

The upper portion of a tapered slab which measures 1.17m in length, .56m in width at its top, .44m in width at its base. The surviving edges - dexter, sinister and top - are chamfered and measure .03m in width. The slab lies near the south wall of the north chapel in the north transept. The decorated surface of the slab is somewhat weathered, but the design is decipherable. It consists of a seven-armed segmental cross carved in relief, with fleur-de-lis terminals. A raised border occurs along the three surviving sides of the slab. There is no evidence to suggest that the slab bore an inscription.

Bibliography: Unpublished.

Site Name	Kilcooly Abbey
Townland	Kilcoolyabbey
SMR Site No.	T1043-03401
N.G.R.	22906/15777

The site and lands for this abbey were granted by Donàl Mor O'Brien in honour of St. Benedict and Mary Virgin to the 'Coarb of Mag Airb' *c.*1182. It was affiliated to Jerpoint in 1184. The dedication of the monastery suggests it was possibly Benedictine until 1184. However, in Henry III's confirmation of the foundation by Donal O'Brien, the dedication is given as that of Blessed Mary only. In 1228 Stephen of Lexington was attacked by robbers near Kilcooley and later deposed the abbot for neglect of duties and the prior was ordered to act under the new English abbot of Jerpoint. In 1341 Thomas O'Rourke was abbot. In 1444 the abbey was almost completely destroyed by armed men and the abbot travelled to England. Around the time of abbot Philip who died in 1463, the abbey was partly rebuilt, with the help of the Butler family. Philip Omulwardayn had become abbot in 1450, after the death of Thomas Bovil, to be later replaced by Malachy Omulrian, formerly a monk of Holycross, who became abbot of Kilcooly in 1464. The abbey was surrendered in 1541 by Thomas Shortall, when its acreage was given as *c.* 700 and the buildings included a church, belfry, hall, dormitory, four chambers, kitchen and stables. In 1557 Kilcooly was granted, along with other monasteries, to Thomas, Earl of Ormond and Ossory. The monastery was reoccupied by monks in the first half of the seventeenth century (Gwynn and Hadcock 1970, 137-8).

Kilcooly abbey, which was built *c.* 1200, is plain in type. Since its destruction in 1445, the nave has lost its two aisles and a new north transept along with a tower was built. The south range of the cloister is a reconstruction, which probably dates to the time of Abbot Philip, who died in 1463 (see slab no. 3) Good quality stonework is attested by the sculpture on the south wall of the south transept where there are two niches featuring carvings of St. Christopher, a Butler shield, and a mermaid holding a mirror accompanied by a fish. The four piers of the crossing tower are built into the original transept openings. Those at the west angles feature an ogee-headed niche in which the grooves of wooden seats remain. The south niche was probably for the abbot, the other for his deputy. There is a six-light, traceried east window in the chancel. The windows in the chapels and in the room over the south transept are of two-lights. The low, broad tower contained dwelling rooms, as did the upper storeys of the north and south transept. In the field in front of the abbey there is a columbarium and a two-storey building - probably an infirmary (Leask 1960, 69-72). The tombs and floor slabs are situated in the chancel.

1. GROUP: 4 Fig. 14s

This tapered slab measures 1.90m in length, .58m in width at its top, .52m in width at its base and .09m in average thickness. All four edges are

chamfered and measure .03m in width. It is secured to the wall of a tomb niche situated in the north wall of the chancel. Its decorated surface is badly worn, and the design is barely decipherable. It consists of a seven-armed segmental cross, carved in relief, with the arms terminating in simple fleurs-de-lis. Three cross-bands occur at the base of the cross-head, surmounting the cross-shaft, which terminates in a pillar-base form. An inscription in Black Letter occurs along both sides and across the top. It is illegible.
Bibliography: Unpublished.

2. GROUP: 4
This rectangular slab measures 2.09m in length, .70m in width and .13m in average thickness. It is secured against the wall of a recess which is located in the north wall of the chancel. Its decorated surface is chipped and weathered. The design consists of a seven-armed segmental cross with fleur-de-lis terminals, carved in relief. A motif, formed of three cross-bands, occurs at the base of the cross-head, surmounting the cross shaft, which terminates in a pillar-base form. An interlocked pair of rectangular forms, open at the base, occupy the central part of the slab. An inscription in Black Letter occurs along both sides of the slab, across the top and along the cross-shaft. It has been transcribed and translated by Carrigan (1903, 455) as:

HIC IACET JOHANNES CATWELL QUODA DUS DE MOYLASSAIN Q' OBIIT I VIGILA SCI/PATRICI A^{O} DO. MO^{O}/CCCCC^{O} XX° II. ET ELICIA STOUC EI' UXOR/RORICUS OTWNYE SCRIPSIT.
(Here lie John Cantwell formerly lord of Moylasssain, who died 16th March, 1532 and Ellis Stoke his wife. Rory O'Tunny wrote this).

Bibliography: Carrigan,Wm., 1903, 455.

3. GROUP: 5 Fig. 35
A tapered slab which measures 1.86m in length, .61m in width at its top, .54m in width at its base and .17m in average thickness. It is secured to the wall of a tomb niche situated in the north wall of the chancel. It survives in good condition. The design on the lower half of the slab consists of the figure of an abbot, carved in false relief, complete with Mass Vestments. Over a voluminous alb he wears a pointed chasuble. 'IHC' is inscribed into the lower part of the alb. With his left hand he holds a book, while he holds a crozier, with an out-turned foliated head in his right. Forming the upper part of the slab is a large shield, bearing the Symbols of the Passion. Above the cross, which occupies the centre of the shield, are the letters 'INRI', inscribed in Roman capitals on a titulus . The cross-beam features two nails and from it is suspended the Crown of Thorns. The ladder, pinchers and the cock standing on the pot occupy the sinister side and the dexter side features the lance, the scourging post, the seamless garment, three dice, two scourges and a hammer. An inscription in Black Letter occurs along both sides, across the top and base of the slab. It has been published by Hunt (1974, cat. no. 242) as follows:

HIC JACET PHILIPP' O'MOLWANAYN QUONDAM ABBAS HUJUS LOCI CUM SUIS PARENTIBUS QUI PLURA OPERA BONA SIPIRITUALIA AND TEMPORALIA FECURUNT QUORUM ANIMABUS PPICIETUR DIEUS ANNO DOMINI MCCCCLXIII.
(Here lies Philip O'Molwanayn, formerly abbot of this house, together with his parents who performed many good works both spiritual and temporal. On whose soul may God have mercy. A.D. 1463).

Bibliography: Hunt, J., 1974, cat. 242, pl. 184.

4. GROUP: 5 Figs. 14d, 36
This tapered limestone slab, with an angled base, measures 1.62m in length, .51m in width at its top, .31m in width at the beginning of angled base, (tapering to .14m in width) and .08m in average thickness. All four edges are chamfered and measure .09m in width. The slab is secured to the north wall of the chancel, between the two tomb niches. Its decorated surface is somewhat worn and chipped. Its top bears a cruciform design carved in relief, in a sunken rectangular panel, surrounded by a narrow border. The design consists of a cross-head, formed of a ring of eight penannular circles, surmounting a short cross-stem. There is no evidence to suggest that the slab bore an inscription.
Bibliography: Unpublished.

5. GROUP: 4
A tapered slab which measures 1.88m in length, .70m in width at its top, .58m in with at its base. It is secured to the wall of a tomb niche which is situated in the south wall of the chancel. The upper sinister corner of the slab is broken off. A number of cracks occur across the face of the slab and it is also badly chipped. The design consists of a seven-armed segmental cross, carved in relief. Each arm terminates in a stylised fleur-de-lis. A motif formed of three cross-bands occurs at the base of the cross-head, surmounting the cross-shaft, which terminates in a pillar-base form. An interlocked pair of rectangular forms, open at the base, occupy the central part of the slab. There is no evidence to suggest that the slab bore an inscription
Bibliography: Unpublished.

6. GROUP: 5 Fig. 37
This tapered slab measures 1.85m in length, .56m in width at its top, .49m in width at its base and .11m in average thickness. All four edges are chamfered and measure 0.02m in width. The slab is secured to the wall of a tomb niche situated in the south wall of the chancel. The decorated surface of the slab is severely worn and chipped. and three cracks occur across its face. The design is carved in relief. The upper portion of the slab features a selection of the Symbols of the Passion. The cup and lance, from which the Crown of Thorns is suspended, act as the cross-head. The hammer occurs on its sinister side and the ladder on the

dexter side. The pinchers, one-piece garment and the scourge occur below these. All the symbols together form the shape of a shield, which surmounts a cross-shaft, featuring foliate forms. The cross terminates in a stepped base. An inscription in Black Letter occurs across the top of the slab and along both its sides. Carrigan (1903, 452) transcribed and translated it as follows:

HIC IACENT DONALDUS OHE/DYAN FILIUS EIUS./ANNO DNI M⁰ CCCC LII.
(Here lies Donnell O'Heydan and his son, A.D. 1452).

Bibliography: Carrigan,Wm., 1903, 452.

Site Name	Kiltinan Church
Townland	Kiltinan
SMR Site No.	T1070-101
N.G.R.	22326/13202

This medieval parish church consisted of a nave and chancel with a crossing tower. It is suggested that the name derives from Cill tSenáin, the church of St. Senan (O'Connor 1991, 10), who was the sixth century patron saint of fishermen in the Shannon estuary. There are many churches in Munster dedicated to him.

Only the north wall survives of the chancel. The tower, which has four floors surviving, is lighted on the south side only by four, single-light, ogee-headed windows. Access from the chancel to the nave, through the tower, is by means of two arches of well-cut limestone. The stairs occur in the east corner of the tower. Two doorways exist at the first floor level, in the east wall of the tower. The first occurs at the south end of the wall and allows access to the chancel and to the inside of the tower; the second occurs at the north end of the east wall. This permits access to the inside of the tower only.

A round-headed doorway survives in both the north and south wall of the nave. The west wall features a plain two-light, round-headed window, which splays inwardly. A single-light, ogee-headed window occurs in the north and south wall. The well-known Kiltinan Sheela-na-gig was originally situated in the south-west angle of the church, forming a quoin, before it was unlawfully removed in 1990.

Kiltinan slabs 1 and 2 stand in the chancel area.

1. GROUP: 1 Fig. 38
This tapered sandstone slab stands 1.11m in height above ground level, .36m in width at its present top, .47m in width at its base and .22m in average thickness. It appears to stand upside down. Its decorated surface, which faces east, is severely weathered and bears some lichen growth. The design is decipherable and consists of three parallel grooves which form a double outline cross-stem. The outer examples emanate from a rectangular panel, while the central groove begins at the top of this panel, thus dividing it. In each of these halves is one short line. The outer grooves of the cross-stem together form the rectangular panel. A grooved border, .25m in width, runs close to the edge of the slab. Only traces of it remain on the sinister side. There is no evidence to suggest that the slab bore an inscription.
Bibliography: Unpublished.

2. GROUP: 1
This tapered sandstone slab stands 1.19m in height above ground level, .35m in width at its top, .48m in width at its base and 0.18m in average thickness. It stands, inverted, north of no. 1. The decorated surface of the slab is badly weathered. It bears a grooved design consisting of three parallel grooves forming a double outlined cross-stem. The head of the slab, if present, is buried beneath ground level. The outer grooves of the cross-stem define an open rectangular area at its base and terminate in simple volutes. Parallel bands in relief occur alongside each volute. A grooved border runs close to the edges of the slab. There is no evidence to suggest that the slab bore an inscription.
Bibliography: Unpublished.

Site Name	Knockgraffon Church
Townland	Knockgraffon
SMR Site No.	T1075-019
N.G.R.	20486/12953

Nothing is on record concerning the history of this site. The church is of nave and chancel type, divided by a pointed arch. The east window of cinquefoil mouldings is thought to be a later insertion. A motte and bailey survive to the south of the church, and a rectangular tower still stands on the bailey. Knockgraffon 1 lies among rubble inside the south wall of the chancel.

1. GROUP: 7
This consists of portion of a limestone slab which measures .69m in length, .54m in width and .25m in average thickness. It lies among other stone fragments in a tomb niche in the south wall of the chancel. The surviving portion of the slab is damaged, with only two original edges: the dexter edge which is chamfered and measures .08m in width; and the upper edge, which is not chamfered. The upper surface of the slab is badly worn, and there is no evidence to suggest that it bore a design. An inscription in Black Letter occurs along the chamfered edge. O'Donovan (1840, 117) read this as:

HIC JACET DOMINUS MATHAEUS KENT QUONDAM RECTOR DE KNOCERAFON A.D. MCCCCCXXXX.
(Here lies Lord Matthew Kent formerly rector of Knockgraffon A.D. 1540).

Bibliography: O'Donovan, J., 1840.

Site Name Liathmore/Leighmore Church
Townland Leigh
SMR Site No. T1042-05503.
N.G.R. 22246/15763

This monastery was founded by St. Mochoemoc, nephew of St. Ita, in the seventh century. The history of the monastery is largely unrecorded, however, the following list of abbots exists: Conghus, died in 752; abbot Egnach mac Erc, died in 767; abbot Reachtabhra, died in 900; abbot Maclenna, who was also abbot of Emly, died in 933 and abbot Conaing mac Finn, who was also abbot of Daire-mor, died in 1014 (Gwynn and Hadcock 1970, 40).

The ruins of two churches stand at this site as well as a complex of grassy mounds which may represent the remains of more structures. The site was excavated by R.A.S. Macalister and H.G. Leask (1945-8, 1-13). The smaller of the two churches, a single-celled structure lies to the north of the monastic site. Its east and west gables are very steep and there are antae to both gables. The west doorway and east windows, which were represented by rough gaps, are now restored. Although the date of this church is unknown, it may be of the same date or later than the earliest part of the larger church (Leask 1955, 66). The constructional history of the latter is quite complicated. The structure as it now stands consists of a nave with a vaulted chancel. The oldest parts of the building are the north and east chancel walls, which originally formed a single-celled church. There were antae at the eastern end. The next phase of building is represented by the addition of a narrow chancel which fitted in between the antae of the original building. All that survives of this chancel is part of its arch, which can be seen in the exterior of the east wall of the church. During the fifteenth century the original nave was converted into a chancel, the east arch was blocked up and a wide nave was added. It was also at this time that the vault, the south wall and the living quarters over the chancel were built. Pieces of twelfth-century carved stonework are built into the south wall of the church. The two grave-slabs lie in the chancel (original church).

1. GROUP: 5 Fig. 39
This tapered sandstone slab measures 1.61m in length, .52m in width at its top, .43m in width at its base and .09m in average thickness. An undercut chamfer measuring .09m in width runs all around the slab. It lies on the ground in the chancel of the church. The slab bears three cracks, one runs diagonally across the lower half of the slab, the other two occur at its head. The design occurs in relief and consists of a badly worn human figure with out-stretched arms, wearing a long robe. Perhaps it represents the Triumphant Christ. There is no evidence to suggest that the slab bore an inscription.
Bibliography: Ó Floinn, R. (forthcoming)

2. GROUP: 7
This rectangular sandstone slab measures 1.73m in length, .50m in width and .08m in average thickness. It lies close to no. 1, in the chancel. Very little of the sinister and dexter edges survive. The upper surface of the slab is badly worn and pitted. There is no evidence to suggest that the slab bore an inscription or design.
Bibliography: Unpublished.

Site Name Lisronagh Church
Townland Lisronagh
SMR Site No. T1077-010
N.G.R. 22039/12921

Lisronagh village is located towards the northern end of the area which formed the Norman rural borough established here in the later twelfth century (Glasscock 1970, 172), probably by William de Burgo. The ecclesiastical taxation returns of 1319-22 evidence the existence of a church at Lisronagh at this time (Barry 1977, 167). A 1333 rental of the manor survives and has been published by Curtis (1935). Barry has suggested that the borough might have had a population of over two hundred and forty inhabitants at this time (1977, 167). Due to its location between Fethard and Clonmel it failed to develop as a true town. Like many such rural boroughs in the south-east of Ireland it features a tower house, known as Howett's Castle, and an adjacent churchyard.

The churchyard is of rectangular plan and in it stand the ruins of a simple rectangular Protestant church which features a tower at its western end. It was built around 1831 (Curtis 1935, 58). There is no apparent trace of the medieval church which stood at this site.

Lisronagh 1, which survives in two portions, is located outside the east gable of the church.

1. GROUP: 4 Fig. 11
This slab survives in two portions, which do not fit together. The upper portion measures .89m in length, .83m in width at its broken base and .12m in average thickness. The sinister edge features a chamfer which measures .03m in width. The portion tapers in form. The top and upper sinister corner of the slab are broken off, but much of the design carved on its upper surface remains. It consists of a seven-armed segmental cross, carved in relief, with simple floriated terminals. Each of the three remaining sunken segments of the cross-head contain motifs: the upper dexter one features an encircled arrangement of a four-legged whirling motif; the lower dexter one features a foliate design; and the lower sinister segment features an interlocked arrangement of four elongated links with rounded ends. An outline lozenge occurs at the crossing of the transom with the shaft. A series of closely set, obliquely disposed, incised lines outline the centre of the cross-head. In each of the surviving external spaces between the cross-arms

(with the exception of the lower dexter one) are foliate designs with tendrils. The lower dexter one contains an incised, outline, compass-drawn motif formed of eight interlocked almond-shaped rings.

The lower portion of the slab measures .64m in length, .77m in width at its top and .70m in width at its base. Both sides feature chamfered edges which measure .12m in width. The decorated upper surface is somewhat worn. The design, which is in relief, consists of the lower portion of a cross-shaft, terminating in a semi-circular base which features a sunken square recess. Beneath this, occupying the lower sinister area, are three further recesses of similar form.
Bibliography: Maher, D., 1992, 30-37.

Site Name	Loughmore Church
Townland	Tinvoher
SMR Site No.	T1035-030
N.G.R.	21151/16719

In the centre of the old graveyard stands the remains of a medieval church divided into a nave and chancel. Both gables and its chancel-arch stand intact but the north and south side - walls have many breaches. The chancel arch is a round-headed one of cut stone. There is a small window high up on the west gable, and the ragged opes of windows survive in the north and south walls of the chancel. There is no trace of an east window. A vaulted building (priests residence?) abuts the east end of the church (Seymour 1908, 461).

Close to the church stands the ruins of Loghmore Court. The south end features the tower of a fifteenth century castle, the remainder is a seventeenth century fortified house. It was the home of the Purcells, and gave its title to Nicholas Purcell, Baron Loughmore. He was one of the Jacobite signatories of the Treaty of Limerick, 1691. The medieval church houses the seventeenth century Purcell monuments (Harbison 1989, 291).

All the medieval grave-slabs lie in the chancel of the church.

1. GROUP: 4
This rectangular slab measures 1.72m in length, .58m in width and .08m in average thickness. It lies in the chancel near the entrance to the vaulted building. Its decorated surface is worn and the design consists of a seven-armed segmental cross. The cross-head is carved in low relief and surmounts an incised outline shaft. The cross-head is very worn and not all of the arm - terminals survive. The outline cross-shaft terminates in a pillar-base form. A border, defined by a single groove, survives on the dexter and sinister sides and across the base. Some of the recessed areas of the cross-head display pock marks. There is no evidence to suggest that the slab bore an inscription.
Bibliography: Unpublished.

Site Name	Marlfield Church
Townland	Inishlounaght
SMR Site No.	T1083-017
N.G.R.	21760/12152

A nineteenth century church stands on the site of this medieval abbey which was probably founded in 1147. The monastery became subject to Monasteranenagh in 1151. Conganus was abbot in the twelfth century. It is possible that Donal Mór O'Brien visited the abbey in 1172. In 1221 the abbot of Midleton became abbot of Inishlounaught without proper authority. Shortly afterwards the monastery became a centre of violent rebellion and it was taken from Monasteranenagh and made subject to Furness in 1227. Rebellion broke out again when the monks refused admittance to a monk from Furness. Stephen of Lexington went to the monastery for three days to restore discipline. In 1230 there were fifty lay brothers and thirty-six monks resident in the abbey. A new colony of monks was sent there from Furness in 1249 to restore authority. In 1278 affiliation to Monasteranenagh was restored. In 1474 Thomas Ogrechain, a vicar, was received into the abbey for the appointment of abbot. In 1540 James Butler surrendered the monastery. He then became dean of Lismore. The abbey was never revived. The modern English name 'Marlfield' was derived from the excellent marl (a deposit of stalagmite) at this site (Gwynn and Hadcock 1970, 135-6).

A new church was afterwards built at this site. The east window (a fifteenth century insertion in the old church) still survives. A transitional doorway of *c.*1200, also survives high up in the west wall of the church. It was probably the doorway leading into the cloister from the aisle of the original church. Surviving in the south wall of the church is a thirteenth century window or tomb niche. (Harbison 1970, 232; Bagwell 1909, 267-8).

There are two slabs of interest at this site. no. 1 forms the threshold of the door leading into the nave; no. 2 is built into a wall south of the church.

1. GROUP: 3 Fig. 14k
This tapered slab survives in two portions which together measure 1.25m in length, .69m in width at the top and .57m in width at the base. Its thickness is unattainable due to its position as a threshold flagstone, between the porch and the church. The two portions survive in a worn condition. The design, which is incised, consists of an outline cross with four trefoil terminals, surmounting a cross-stem which terminates in a stepped base. A Lombardic inscription occurs along the sinister side of the slab. It reads:

HIC IACET MA...I(G?) . AICIET':DS:.
(Here lies [the rest is unintelligible]).

Bibliography: Unpublished.

2. GROUP: 4 Fig. 40
This tapered slab measures 1.86m in length, .49m in width at its top and .46m in width at its base. Its thickness is unattainable, as the slab is built into a

wall. The decorated surface is rather worn and the sinister side is partly broken. The limestone is of poor quality. A design, carved in relief, consists of a seven-armed segmental cross featuring a fleur-de-lis at each arm terminal. Three simple cross-bands occur at the base of the cross-head surmounting the cross-shaft, which terminates in a stepped base. A raised border occurs along the dexter and sinister sides, parallel to the cross-shaft. A partly obliterated border occurs along the top of the slab. An inscription in Black Letter occurs along the sinister side. The first word is in relief, however, the rest is incised. It survives in a worn condition, especially towards its lower end. The following is legible:

HIC IACET PIUS V(I)(R) D(U?)S LIIBA..ER.....
(Here lies Pius, noble husband?).

Bibliography: Unpublished.

Site Name	Old St. Mary's, Clonmel
Townland	Burgagery-Lands West
SMR Site No.	T1083-019
N.G.R.	22026/12237

This church was dedicated to the Assumption of the Blessed Virgin Mary. No sign of its original fabric exists. However, with the extensive re-building of the church in 1857, a number of discoveries were made and the entire area beneath the old floor was discovered to be paved with grave-slabs.

The early thirteenth century church was associated with the Augustinian priory of Athassel. It had a nave, aisles, a long chancel and possibly transepts. The graceful arcade, high-pitched roof and clustered column were replaced by a less dignified fourteenth-century structure, comprising a nave, chancel and aisles. The north aisle had five bays, the south four and a tower. The aisles were rather narrow and it seems that the tower was raised on the site of the south transept of the earlier church.

The pair of windows in the chancel and west front survive from the medieval church up to the present day. Along with the loss of the old church was the destruction of many ancient monuments. Most of the main Clonmel families had their burial places within the church. Among these were the Whites, Walls, Barons, Leynachs, Daniels, Stritches and Brennocks.

In 1805 the church was heavily repaired. The chancel was shortened by twenty-nine feet. A new porch was constructed at the west end and the top storey of the tower was replaced by an octangular pile. Inside, the 'patron' gallery, on the north side, and the Corporation gallery, on the south side, were taken down.

The church was almost entirely rebuilt in 1857 by Mr. Welland. The only features surviving today from the old work include the lower storey of the tower, the east and west windows, the chancel arch, the three-light window of the porch (originally belonging to the White mortuary chapel) and the walls of the aisles (Burke 1907, 263-98).

The seventeenth century grave-slabs are located inside the church as floor slabs while Cat. no's 1, 2 and 3 are situated outside the church to the north.

1. GROUP: 5 Fig. 41
A rectangular slab which measures 2.18m in length, .82m in width and .37m in average thickness. An undercut chamfer exists on both edges of the slab and measures .13m in width. It is located outside of the church, standing against the north wall. Its decorated surface is worn and chipped, though the design is easily decipherable. It consists of a ringed cross with bifid terminals. Emanating out from the angles are four diagonally disposed arms, with expanded terminals. The cross-head surmounts a fluted cross-shaft, which tapers slightly towards the top. It terminates in an elaborate pillar-base form. An heraldic shield occurs on either side of the cross-shaft, but there is no evidence to suggest that they bore any charges. An inscription in Black Letter occurs along the top of the slab and on both its sides. Hewetson (1902, 256-7) transcribes and translated the inscription as follows:

HIC JACET TERRENTIUS O/DONILL QUI OBIT 4 MARTI 1583 ET EJUS UXOR ELANA HUETT QUAE OBIIT 24/APRILIS 1591? EORUM FILII QUI HUNC TUMULU/FIERI FECERNT AO 1592 QUIB' SIT PROPITIUS OMNIPOTENS AMEN.
(Here lies Terence O'Donill who died 4 March 1583 and his wife Helena? Huett who died 24 April 1591. Also all their sons who caused this tomb to be made in the year 1592, to whom may the Almighty be propitious. Amen).

Bibliography: Hewetson, 1902, 255-8.

2. GROUP: 4
A tapered slab which measures 1.61m in length, .75m in width at its top, .64m in width at its base and .08m in average thickness. All four edges are chamfered and measure .03m in width. It lies on the ground, outside the east side of the church. Its decorated surface is severely worn and portions of the sinister and basal edges are broken. The design, which only partially survives, consists of a seven-armed segmental cross, carved in relief, with each arm terminating in a fleur-de-lis. The cross-shaft terminates in a pillar-base form which features a skull and cross-bones. An inscription in Roman lettering occurs along the base of the slab. It reads:

MEM(E)NTO MORI
(Remember Death!).

Bibliography: Unpublished.

3. GROUP: 4 Fig. 42
This consists of a rectangular slab which measures 1.50m in height above ground level, .70m in width and .17m in average thickness. It stands facing east in the graveyard, north of the church. The decorated surface of the slab is worn and its upper sinister corner is broken. The design consists of a seven-armed segmental cross, carved in relief, with

each arm terminating in a fleur-de-lis. Three cross-bands occur at the base of the cross-head, surmounting the cross-shaft. The base of the cross is buried. An inscription in Black Letter occurs along both sides, and survives in a somewhat worn condition. Only the following is decipherable (on the dexter side):

A DNI M CCCCC (XX?)....DIE'..../.
(A.D. 1520?)

Bibliography: Unpublished.

Site Name	St. Dominick's Church, Cashel
Townland	St. Dominick's Abbey
SMR Site No.	T1061-025
N.G.R.	20758/14070

St. Dominick's Priory was founded in 1243 by David O'Kelly, a Dominican of Cork. In 1480, a later archbishop, John Cantwell, was recognised as patron and co-founder as he rebuilt the friary after a fire. In 1535-6 Edward Brown, the prior, leased out some of the property and in 1540 he surrendered the friary. The friary had a church and belfry, a chamber with two cellars and a dorter. The friary was granted to Walter Fleming in 1543-4 (Gwynn and Hadcock 1970, 223).

St. Dominick's, was one of the first Dominican churches to be built in Ireland. The church is of the usual friars' type, consisting of a long rectangle. To it was added a large south wing with a west aisle, *c.*1270. The church had a number of thirteenth century lancet windows which were replaced by traceried windows *c.*1450. In the south wall of the choir there is a row of nine lancets with plain sandstone dressings, an early example of piers and lights which became popular later in the century. The east wall has three lancets of the same date. No trace remains of the claustral buildings which lay to the north. The tower is plain and spans the width of the church, but it is narrow from west to east (Leask 1958, 93).

The medieval grave-slabs are lying in the nave and in the south wing.

1. GROUP: 5

This tapered slab survives in four portions which are presently joined together by cement. It measures 1.77m in length, .50m in width at its top, .36m in width at its base and .08m in average thickness. It lies in the nave of the church near the north wall. Its decorated surface is weathered, though the design is still decipherable. Apart from the four breaks in the slab, its top edge is broken. The design consists of an incised outline cross. The upper part of the cross-head is missing but it appears to have originally consisted of an outline circle which enclosed four smaller ones, only two of which survive intact. The lower halves of the upper two are also present. Beneath the cross-head is another small circle, which surmounts the cross-stem. The latter terminates in a three-lobed motif. There is no evidence to suggest that the slab bore an inscription.

Bibliography: Unpublished.

2. GROUP: 5 Fig. 14l

This tapered slab, which survives in six portions, measures 2.06m in length, .60m in width at its top, .26m in width at its base and .08m in average thickness. The base of the slab is badly broken and its decorated surface is worn. It lies in the nave near the north wall. The design consists of a cross-head, contained within an outline circle, which surmounts an outline cross-shaft on either side of which are incised designs. The cross-head consists of a simple outline cross with large, three-lobed terminals set within a cusped outline. The outline circle which encloses the cross-head rests on the cross-shaft. An outline knop, occurs at the base of the cross-head and surmounts the cross-shaft which terminates at the base in a large outlined, three-lobed motif. On the sinister side of the cross-shaft is an incised herring-bone pattern. Traces of a matching design survive on its dexter side, separated from it by an outline stem with a circular expansion near its top. Linked to this are a number of incised lines. There is no evidence to suggest that the slab bore an inscription.

Bibliography: Unpublished.

3. GROUP: 6

This rectangular slab measures 1.99m in length and .48m in width. It lies near the north wall of the nave. Its decorated surface is weathered, cracked and chipped. The surviving design consists of an incised outline cross-stem. There is no evidence to suggest that the slab bore a medieval inscription. However, a modern inscription of eighteenth or nineteenth century date occurs on the upper portion of the slab; only a portion of it is legible. It reads:

HERE LIES (THE)/BODY OF (W?)ILL H.....

Perhaps the application of this inscription might have resulted in the obliteration of the cross-head design.

Bibliography: Unpublished.

4. GROUP: 7

The upper half of a tapered slab which measures 1.14m in length, .63m in width at its top and .50m in width at its base. The sinister, dexter and top edges are chamfered and measure .07m in width. It lies near the south wall of the nave. The upper surface of the slab is weathered and there is no evidence to suggest that the slab bore a design or inscription.

Bibliography: Unpublished.

5. GROUP: 7

The lower portion of a tapered slab which measures 1.48m in length, .65m in width at its top, .52m in width at its base and .06m in average thickness. It lies in the nave near the south wall. The upper surface of the slab is weathered. There is no evidence to suggest that the slab bore an inscription or design.

Bibliography: Unpublished.

6. GROUP: 7
This tapered slab measures 1.80m in length, .54m in width at its head, .38m in width at its base and .08m in average thickness. It lies in the nave near the tower. Its upper surface is worn and its edges are chipped. There is no evidence to suggest that the slab bore an inscription or design.
Bibliography: Unpublished.

7. GROUP: 5
This rectangular slab measures 2.06m in length, .51m in width and .08m in average thickness. It lies near the east wall of the south wing. Its decorated surface is somewhat weathered. The design consists of an incised outline cross-stem, which extends the length of the slab, terminating at each end in a fleur-de-lis. A single cross-band surmounts the fleur-de-lis at one end of the slab. An inscription in Lombardic lettering occurs towards one end, on the dexter side of the shaft. The inscription, which is difficult to decipher, except for a few letters, is preceded by an equal-armed cross. The inscription runs in two parallel lines:

(M?).I.A.IE....
A.G....(M?).... .

Bibliography: Unpublished.

8. GROUP: 7
This tapered slab which survives in two portions measures 1.48m in length, 0.52m in width at its head, 0.40m in width at its base and 0.08m in average thickness. It lies near the south wall of the south wing. As well as its fragmentary condition the upper surface of the slab is rather worn. There is no evidence to suggest that the slab bore an inscription or design.
Bibliography: Unpublished.

9. GROUP: 5 Fig. 43
A broken tapered slab which measures 1.43m in length, .59m in width at its top and .43m in width at its base. The slab lies beneath the base of a pillar in the south wall of the south wing. The sinister edge and the base are chamfered and measure .08m in width. The upper portion of the slab is missing and its decorated surface is weathered, however, the incised outline design is easily decipherable. Of the cross-head only the lower portion survives; on the dexter side the lower half of a cross arm with a single-lobed terminal survives and at the base of the cross-head there are two arms with single-lobed terminals. Directly beneath the cross-head is a circle from which the cross-stem emanates. It terminates in a three-lobed motif. There is no evidence to suggest that the slab bore an inscription.
Bibliography: Unpublished

Site Name	St. John's Cathedral, Cashel
Townland	Loghnafina
SMR Site No.	T1061-025
N.G.R.	20758/14070

This Church of Ireland cathedral of St. John the Baptist was completed in 1784. It stands on the site of a medieval parish church of the same name of which no trace survives. The churchyard is partly surrounded by a section of the fourteenth - century city wall. Four effigies, two known as the Hackett effigies, are built into this wall (Hunt 1974, cat. 230-233). They derive from the site of the Old Franciscan Abbey. Also to be seen in the churchyard is the well-known Bolton library, which was once the chapterhouse.

The grave-slabs are set along the edge of the gravel path on the south side of the cathedral. They all date to the seventeenth century except one, which is undated, St. John's Cathedral 1.

1. GROUP: 4
A rectangular slab which measures 1.97m in length and .50m in width. Its thickness is unattainable. The dexter, top and base edges are chamfered and measure .05m in width. The slab lies among others, directly south of the west door of the church. Its decorated surface is very worn. The design consists of a seven-armed segmental cross in low relief, with a fleur-de-lis at each arm terminal. A single cross-band occurs at the base of the cross-head, surmounting the cross-shaft. A similar feature occurs at the base of the cross-shaft surmounting a calvary-like base. A border in low relief, which measures .10m in width, exists on the dexter side and across the top and base of the slab. A panel measuring .16m in width extends from the dexter side, right across the slab, directly beneath the upper cross-band. It seems that the original sinister edge does not survive, as there is no border on this side, the edge is not chamfered and two arm-terminals on this side do not survive. There is no evidence to suggest that the slab bore an inscription.
Bibliography: Unpublished.

Site Name	St. Patrick's Cathedral, Cashel
Townland	St. Patrick's Rock
SMR Site No.	T1061-025
N.G.R.	20758/14070

Cashel was the seat of the Kings of Munster. It is tradition that St. Patrick baptised Cengus, the King of Munster, on the rock. The Kingship of Cashel was taken by Cormac mac Cuilenáin in 901. In 1101 a synod was held at Cashel, over which Muirchertach O'Brien presided, as King of Munster. At this synod Muirchertach granted Cashel of the Kings to the religious of Ireland in general. In 1111, Cashel became the second archbishopric of Ireland, along with Armagh in the north. He resigned after a few years. Domnall O'Longargáin was archbishop at the Synod of Kells in 1152. Matthew O h-Enna was archbishop from 1186-1206. A cathedral was probably built on the rock in either 1101 or 1111. Shortly afterwards Cormac Mac Carthaig built Cormac's Chapel. Domnall Mór O'Brien rebuilt the earlier cathedral in 1169. A more ambitious Gothic cathedral was built in the thirteenth century by three successive archbishops. It is the ruins of this building that can be seen on the Rock today. The buildings on the Rock of Cashel passed into Protestant hands under Queen Elizabeth, when Myler Magrath was archbishop (1571-1622) (Gwynn and Hadcock 1970, 62-3).

The cathedral has a nave, chancel, a crossing tower, two transepts and a residential tower at the western end of the church. The chancel represents the earliest building phase and probably dates to 1230 - the episcopate of Marianus O'Brien (Leask 1958, 90). There are five lancet windows in the south and north wall. The east windows have gone. The south transept may be attributed to Archbishop MacKelly who died in 1252. The north transept, nave, and crossing tower were probably built by Archbishop Mac Carwill around 1260. The residential, strongly fortified tower at the western end of the church was built by Archbishop O'Hedigan for himself. The nave is narrower than the chancel and it is very short. The north and south walls feature entrance archways. The south porch, which is vaulted, has a fifteenth century inserted doorway. There is no north porch.

The medieval slabs are located lying in the chancel. There are also a number of tombs situated in the transept chapels and one in a tomb niche in the south wall of the nave (Leask 1958, 89-93).

1. GROUP: 2 Figs. 14b, 44
This tapered slab measures 1.47m in length, .50m in width at its top, .36m in width at its base and .12m in average thickness. All four edges bear a chamfer which measures .03m in width, now damaged. The slab is located in the Vicar's Choral, lying on limestone blocks. Its decorated surface is somewhat weathered and bears one crack across its centre and a smaller one on the upper dexter side. The design consists of an incised floriated cross with a lozenge-shaped centre, which surmounts a narrow outline cross-stem featuring a circular knop near its top. The cross terminates in a stepped base. A human head is carved in high relief above the cross-head. His hair is dressed in curls below the ears. An inscription in Lombardic lettering occurs along the sinister side and has been transcribed by Hunt (1974, cat. 235) as follows:

H (or *P*) *ARES: AREVI.*

I would transcribe the initial letter as '*P*'.
Bibliography: Hunt, J., 1974, cat. 235.

2. GROUP: 4
A rectangular slab which measures 2.10m in length, .71m in width and .13m in average thickness. It lies in a recess in a side chapel of the south transept. The decorated surface of the slab is somewhat weathered and the lower sinister portion is broken. The design consists of a seven-armed segmental cross in relief, with each arm terminating in a fleur-de-lis. Three cross-bands occur at the base of the cross-head surmounting the cross-shaft. A similar feature occurs at the base of the shaft surmounting an elaborate pillar-base form. An interlocked pair of rectangular forms, open at the base, occupy the centre of the slab. A Black Letter inscription occurs along the sinister and dexter edges and on the cross base. It was transcribed and translated by Fitzgerald (1903, 447) as follows:

HIC JACET PATRICI' CONNOLLIE BURGENSIS VILLE DE CASSELL ET JOHANA/WALE/EIUS UXOR QUE OBIIT DECIO DIE MENS'.... ANO 1506 PATRI' / OBIIT / DIE __ MES' __ Å DNI __.

(Here lies Patrick Connolly burgess of the town of Cashel and Joanna Wale his wife, who died on the 10th day of the month of __ the year 1506. Patrick .... died __ day, month of __ A.D. __.).

Bibliography: Fitzgerald, W., 1903, 447.

3. GROUP: 4
A rectangular slab which measures 2.28m in length, .60m in surviving width at its top and .52m in surviving width at its base. It lies in a recess in a side chapel on the east side of the south transept. The dexter edge of the slab does not survive. The design consists of a seven-armed segmental cross in relief, with each arm terminating in a fleur-de-lis. The horizontal arm on the dexter side does not survive. The cross terminates at base in an elaborate pillar-base form, and an interlocked pair of rectangular forms, open at the base, occupy the central part of the slab. An inscription in Black Lettering occurs along the top of the slab, down the sinister side and across its base. Fitzgerald (1903, 447) transcribed this inscription as follows:

HIC JACET / MAGIST JERIMER' RYAN QUODA OFFICIALIS CASS', ET BONE FAME MIR VUMA(?).

To this reading the following words can be added:

...TAK(P?)ILK / QUE (PUIO)? OBIIT 7 JUNO.

(Here lies / Master Jeremy Ryan formerly official of Cashel and his good wife, (a woman of good repute, his widow)? .... / and .... died 7th June).

Bibliography: Fitzgerald, W., 1903, 447.

4. GROUP: 4 Fig. 45
A rectangular slab which measures 1.98m in length, .72m in width and .06m in average thickness. It lies in the chancel near the south wall. One crack occurs across the face of the slab, at the base of the cross-head. The design consists of a seven-armed segmental cross in relief, with each arm terminating in a stylised fleur-de-lis. A motif formed of three cross-bands occurs at the base of the cross-head, surmounting the cross-shaft. A similar motif occurs at the base of the shaft just above an elaborate pillar-base form. An inscription in Black Lettering occurs along both sides and ends and continues along the cross-shaft. It was transcribed by Fitzgerald (1903, 440) as follows:

HIC JACET EDUS CONNOIRE BURGES' DE CASS' Q OBIIT DIE JUNII ANNO DNI MCCCCCXX PRIMO / ET HONORIA INY CABISSY CI UX' / Q OBIIT XXVIII DIE APLIS A DNI M^{o}CCCCC^{o} XX IIII ET DNS MATHE' CONNOIRE FILI' EOR^{l} Q OBIIT / DIE MES' __

A⁰ DNI M⁰ V __ / QUOR' AIABUS PPICIET' DE' PA ET AVE.
(Here lies Edward Connoire burgess of Cashel who died VI day of June A.D. 1520 / and Honoria Casey his wife / who died 28th day of April A.D. 1524 and Mr. Matthew Connoire their son who died ... / God be merciful to their souls pater and ave.)
Bibliography: Fitzgerald, W., 1903, 440.

5. GROUP: 5 Fig. 46
This rectangular slab measures 2.07m in length and .53m in width. The edges of its sides and base are chamfered and measure .02m in width. It lies in the chancel. The decorated surface is somewhat weathered and it bears a number of cracks. One runs across the centre, another across the lower portion and two occur on the dexter side of the upper portion. The design, which is in relief, consists of a cross with each arm ending in elaborate and florid multi-foiled terminals. The lower element on the dexter arm is absent because of the crack. The arms emanate from a lozenge-shaped centre, which features four triangular segments surrounding a circular one. Three cross-bands occur at the base of the cross-head, separating the cross from its shaft. The shaft terminates in a well-preserved pillar-base form. An inscription in Black Lettering occurs along the edges of the slab and continues along either side of the shaft. It has been transcribed by Fitzgerald (1903, 441) as:

MILLIO CCCCC / XXIIII SUB ISTO LAPIDE TUMULATA EST HONORIA HACKETT DICTI DAVIDI(?) UXOR' QUE DECCESSIT DIE / MENSIS CON.... CUTUS MIORIBUS CU MAIDRIBUS JP.... SEPEIUNT SPRETIS COLLEGIALIBUS/.
ROBERTUS HACKETT ARCH' DACON' CASSELIE. INTESTATUS DECESSIT DECEM DIE DECEMBRIS.
ANN' TUC MILLEN' ET... CENTUS DENIIS ERAT ATER TRIMOS DO.... INCARNACOIS.
(Under this stone lies buried Honoria Hackett, wife of the said David. She died __ 1524 [defies translation] {*Sepeliunt Pretis Collegialibus* - this may be referring to some kind of common fund or guild used to finance Honoria's funeral}
Robertus Hackett, Archdeacon of Cashel, died intestate on the 10th day of December (1510?)).

The rest is unintelligible, however "*erat ater*" perhaps should be "*erat pater*" - he was father.

Trimos - perhaps a form of *Trimus* - three years old - perhaps it is a reference to a surviving three-year old son or daughter, who survived Robert Hackett.
Bibliography: Fitzgerald, W., 1903, 441.

6. GROUP: 4 Fig. 47
This rectangular slab measures 1.82m in length, .59m in width and .08m in average thickness. It lies in the chancel. The decorated surface is rather worn, though the design is easily decipherable. One crack occurs across the face of the slab at its lower end. The design consists of a seven-armed segmental cross in relief with simple fleur-de-lis terminals. A motif formed of three cross-bands occurs at the base of the cross-head, surmounting the shaft. The cross terminates in an elaborate pillar-base form. An inscription in Black Lettering occurs along the two sides and ends and along portion of the cross-shaft. The inscription was transcribed and translated by Fitzgerald (1903, 436) as:

HIC JACET EDVARDUS FILIUS THOME BUTLER QUI OBIIT XXIII DIE MENSIS SEPTEMB' ANNO / DNI M CCCCC XX III / ET MARGARET COMYN / EIUS UXOR BAMC TUBAM FIERI FECIT INBIBENTES UT NEMO ALIEN' BIC SEPULIETUR QUOR / AIABUS DE PPICIET ˉ AMEN PAT ET AVE.
(Here lies Edward son of Thomas Butler who died on the 23rd day of September A.D. 1503, and Margaret Comyn his wife who caused this tomb to be made, both forbidding that any stranger should be here buried. God be merciful to their souls pater and ave).

In my opinion this date should be 1523 (see Latin version) .
Bibliography: Fitzgerald, W., 1903, 435-6..

7. GROUP: 4(?)
The lower half of a rectangular slab which measures 1.10m in length, .57m in width at its top, .51m in width at its base and .09m in average thickness. It lies in the chancel. The decorated surface of the slab is weathered. The surviving design consists of the lower portion of a cross-shaft, featuring three cross-bands above a pillar-base form. Portion of an inscription in Black Lettering occurs along the dexter and sinister sides. It survives in a worn condition. Fitzgerald (1903, 439) transcribed and translated the inscription as:

[IACO]BI CATUELL QUI OBIIT QUARTO DIE NOUEMBRIS / EIUS UXOR QUI OBIIT .....
(Jacob Cantwell who died the 4th day of November .... his wife who died ....).
Bibliography: Fitzgerald, W., 1903, 439.

8. GROUP: 6
The lower portion of a tapered slab which measures 1.10m in length, .57m in width at its top, .51m in width at its base and .09m in average thickness. It lies in the chancel near the south wall. The decorated surface of the slab is very worn, and only traces of two parallel grooves, representing the cross-stem, survive. There is no evidence to suggest that the slab bore an inscription.
Bibliography: Fitzgerald, W., 1903, 439, no. 13.

9. GROUP: 4 Fig. 48
The upper portion of a rectangular slab which measures .59m in length, .75m in width. It lies in the chancel near the south wall. The decorated surface of the slab is worn and the upper sinister corner is broken, however, the design is easily decipherable. It consists of the head of a seven-armed cross, cut in relief. Each arm terminates in a stylised fleur-de-lis. At the centre of the cross-head

is an incised outline cross. There is no evidence to suggest that the slab bore an inscription.
Bibliography: Fitzgerald, W., 1903, 439, no. 14.

10. GROUP: 6
This consists of a tapered slab with a missing base, which measures 1.43m in length, .59m in width at its head, .41m in width at its base and .06m in average thickness. It lies in the chancel, near the east window. Its decorated surface is somewhat weathered and the slab is broken into three portions. All that survives of the design is an incised, outline cross-stem. An inscription in Lombardic Lettering occurs on the dexter and sinister sides of the slab face. It is very worn and is difficult to decipher, except for the following letters on its dexter side:

....V.O....IIT..T.... .

Bibliography: Unpublished.

11. GROUP: 4
This fragmentary tapered slab measures 2.01m in length, .87m in width at its top and .75m in width at its base. It lies in the chancel and survives in poor condition. The upper portion of the slab is cracked on the dexter side and its lower portion has only a few fragments surviving. These are cemented into position. Only the upper portion of the design, which is in relief, survives. It consists of a seven-armed segmental cross, with each arm terminating in a fleur-de-lis. Three simple cross-bands separate the shaft from the cross-head. An inscription in Black Lettering occurs on the two sides and ends and on either side of the cross-shaft. It has been transcribed and translated by Fitzgerald (1903, 439) as:

HIC IACET PETRUS CANTUUELL FILIUS....
Q OBIIT.... / POLTILIBAN ET O' ICESTO.

The following can also be added to the above:

.... ET OWLKEIN MENSIS.

(Here lies Peter Cantwell son of __ who died __).

The rest is unintelligible.
Bibliography: Fitzgerald, W., 1903, 439.

12. GROUP: 6
This broken tapered slab measures 1.86m in length, .59m in width at its top, .38m in width at its base and .06m in average thickness. It lies in the chancel near the east window. The slab bears a number of breaks across its face and its lower sinister side; it is chipped and spalled. Its decorated surface is weathered and only traces of the design are decipherable. All that survives is the remains of an incised outline cross-stem on the lower portion of the slab. There is no evidence to suggest that the slab bore an inscription.
Bibliography: Fitzgerald, W., 1903, 437, no. 4.

13. GROUP: 4
This tapered slab measures 1.96m in length, .78m in width at its head and .72m in width at its base. It lies in the chancel near the south wall and is cracked across its centre and twice across its lower end. Its decorated surface is weathered. The design consists of a seven-armed segmental fleur-de-lis cross, carved in relief. A broad cross-band occurs at the base of the cross-head and surmounts the cross-shaft. A similar feature occurs at the base of the shaft. The cross terminates in a pillar-base form. An inscription in Black Lettering occurs on the dexter and sinister edges. Unfortunately its weathered state renders the inscription illegible. However, Fitzgerald (1903, 437) deciphered the following from the lower dexter corner of the slab:

....FILIUS PETRI HEDIAN.....

(Son of Peter Hayden).

Bibliography: Fitzgerald, W., 1903, 437.

14. GROUP: 4
This tapered slab measures 1.93m in length, .85m in width at its top, .59m in width at its base and .08m in average thickness. It lies in the chancel. The decorated surface of the slab is somewhat worn, though the design is decipherable. A seven-armed segmental cross, carved in relief, occupies the centre of the slab. Each arm terminates in a simple fleur-de-lis. Three cross-bands occur at the base of the cross-head, surmounting the cross-shaft, and a similar grouping occurs at the base of the shaft. The cross terminates in a stepped base. An inscription in Black Lettering runs along the dexter and sinister sides. Fitzgerald (1903, 443) transcribed and translated the inscription as:

HIC IACET DANIELUS JUCCOIGBE IURIS PERITUS AC CASSELL BURGENSIS / (QUI OBIIT) .... MENSE / MARTII ANNO DNI M (CCCCC) 88.

(Here lies Daniel Jacobs skilled lawyer and burgess of Cashel who died in the month of March, A.D. 1588).

Bibliography: Fitzgerald, W., 1903, 443.

15. GROUP: 4 Fig. 49
This tapered slab measures 2m in length, .58m in width at its top, .53m in width at its base and .10m in average thickness. It lies near the north wall of the chancel. The decorated surface of the slab is somewhat weathered. Two cracks run across the slab face and the top sinister corner is broken. The design consists of a seven-armed segmental cross, carved in relief, with each arm terminating in a fleur-de-lis. Three cross-bands occur at the base of the cross-head, surmounting the cross-shaft. The cross terminates in a pillar-base form. Superimposed on the cross-shaft is a shield, possibly that of the Archdeacon family. An inscription in Black Lettering occurs along the dexter and sinister sides and across the base. It survives in a weathered condition and has been transcribed and translated by Fitzgerald (1903, 444) as follows:

RICARDUS ARCDEKE ECCLIE .... PCURATOR BUI' ET TRESAURARI' MEUS EST FABRICATOR CUI / PVIDECIA BAC ECCLIAM / ORNAVIT ET ES' FRUCTU ANNAIE I MULTIS AMPLIAVIT .....

(My maker is Richard Archdeken proctor and treasurer of this church whose forethought adorns this church and in many ways augmented its annual revenue....).

Bibliography: Fitzgerald, W., 1903, 444-5.

16. GROUP: 4 Fig. 50
This rectangular slab measures 1.85m in length, .60m in width and .10m in average thickness. It lies in the chancel. Its decorated surface is worn, cracked and broken. It bears a seven-armed segmental cross carved in relief, with the arms terminating in fleurs-de-lis. The cross terminates in a pillar-base form. A motif, probably to be interpreted as a heraldic rose, is carved in relief on either side of the cross-shaft. An inscription in Black Lettering occurs along the two sides, across the top and base of the slab and along either side of the cross-shaft. It is worn in places. Fitzgerald (1903, 442) transcribed and translated the inscription as follows:

HIC IACET JOBES CONRAN CLERICUS QUONDAM __ / __ QUI OBIIT / __ DIE ANNO DNI QU' AIE PPICIETUR DE' / AMEN..
(Here lies Jobe Conran formerly a cleric .... / .... who died / __ A.D. on whose soul may God have mercy).

Bibliography: Fitzgerald, W., 1903; 442

17. GROUP: 4 Fig. 51
The upper portion of a rectangular slab which measures .87m in length and .82m in width. Its decorated surface is somewhat weathered and it bears one crack on the dexter side. The design consists of a seven-armed segmental cross with fleur-de-lis terminals, carved in relief. Only the top of the cross-shaft survives. Portion of a Black Letter inscription survives on both the sinister and dexter sides. It reads:

"HIC JACET / AIT".
(Here lies / AIT)

Bibliography: Unpublished.

18. GROUP: 4
A tapered slab which measures 1.93m in length, .66m in width at its top, .44m in surviving width at its base and .05m in average thickness. Both sides and ends bear a chamfer which measures .03m in width. It lies in the chancel near the south wall. The lower dexter corner is broken, as is the centre of the slab. Its decorated surface is also somewhat weathered. The design consists of a seven-armed segmental cross, carved in relief, with a simple fleur-de-lis at each arm terminal. Three cross-bands occur at the base of the cross-head, surmounting the cross-shaft which terminates in a stepped base. An inscription in Black Lettering occurs along the sides and ends of the slab. It is poorly preserved. Fitzgerald (1903, 439) transcribed and translated the inscription as:

HIC IACET .... DE CASSELL QUI OBIIT / SEPTIMO .... / .... ANNO DNI MILLIMO CCCCC .... [CUIUS AIE PPICIETUR DEUS] AMEN PATER ET AVE.
(Here lies .... of Cashel who died / September .... / .... A.D. 1500? .... on whose soul may God have mercy Amen. Pater and Ave.).

Bibliography: Fitzgerald,W., 1903, 439.

19. GROUP: 4 Fig. 52
This rectangular slab measures 2.03m in length, .51m in width and .05m in average thickness. A chamfer, measuring .02m in width, exists on its dexter side and upper edge. It lies in the chancel, near the south wall. The decorated surface is somewhat weathered and it bears one crack, which runs across the slab face, and another which occurs on the dexter side of the cross-head. The design, which is in relief, consists of a seven-armed segmental cross, with each arm terminating in a simple fleur-de-lis. Three cross-bands occur at the base of the cross-head surmounting the cross-stem. The base of the cross does not survive, except for one cross-band which probably surmounted its base. An inscription, in Black Lettering, occurs on the dexter and sinister sides, across the top and along either side of the cross-shaft. This is somewhat worn and has been transcribed and translated by Fitzgerald (1903, 438) as:

HIC IACET PATRICIUS O'KEARNY CIVIS CASESSELL' QUI OBIIT VICESIMO SEPTIMO MESIS / MARCII DIE QUI TUMS / .... ECCLIA CASSELLIE EI CORPUS FOUET ANTE ALTARE BRIGIDE E TUBA QUA TENET / SUB LAPIDE MEDIO UBI IACENT TUNC (?) JPE CU HONORIA ET PATRICI KEARNY. O IECTOR BENIGNE QUESO NUC DEVOTE PRO EIUS AIA DIC PATER ET AVE.
(Here lies Patrick O'Kearny, citizen of Cashel, who died on the 27th day of March [....who was buried?] in the church of Cashel, his body rests before the altar of Brigid, and the tomb which he occupies [ ] under the middle stone where they lie he is with Honoria and Patrick Kearny. Now, gentle, reader, I devoutly beseech you to say for his soul a pater and ave).

Bibliography: Fitzgerald, W., 1903, 438-9.

20. GROUP: 4(?)
The lower portion of a rectangular slab which measures 1.57m in length, .67m in width and .05m in average thickness. It lies in the chancel. The decorated surface of the slab is somewhat weathered. One crack occurs across the slab face. The surviving design consists of the cross-shaft which features a single cross-band surmounting a stepped base. An inscription in Black Lettering occurs along the two sides and across the base. Fitzgerald (1903, 437) transcribed and translated it as follows:

HIC IACET JACOBUS BOITON CIVIS CIVITATIS CAS / DNI MILLIO QUGINTESIO XIII ET DAVID' BOITON EIUS FILIUS / ME FIERI FECIT.
(Here lies James Boyton citizen of Cashel .... died 1513 and David Boyton his son who caused this monument to be erected).

Bibliography: Fitzgerald, W., 1903, 437.

21. GROUP: 4
This tapered slab measures 1.97m in length, .68m in width at its top, .41m in width at its base and .07m in average thickness. It lies in the chancel, near the north wall. The decorated surface of the

slab is somewhat worn, however, the design is decipherable and consists of a seven-armed segmental cross, carved in relief, with fleur-de-lis terminals. The cross-shaft features two single cross-bands one at the top and one at the base, which is of pillar-base form. There is no evidence to suggest that the slab bore an inscription.
Bibliography: Fitzgerald, W., 1903, 439.

22. GROUP: 6
This tapered slab measures 1.89m in length, .66m in width at its top, .41m in width at its base and .08m in average thickness. It lies in the chancel near the north wall. Two breaks occur in the upper portion of the slab. The decorated surface of the upper portion of the slab is very worn, but elsewhere the design, which is incised, is decipherable. It extends half of the way up the slab and consists of two broad parallel panels with pointed ends. There is no evidence to suggest that the slab bore an inscription.
Bibliography: Unpublished..

23. GROUP: 4 Fig. 53
The lower portion of a rectangular slab which measures .95m in length, .71m in width and .07m in average thickness. It lies in the chancel near the east window. The design, which is in relief, consists of the lower half of a cross-shaft, terminating in two cross-bands of unequal length, which surmount a pillar-base form. An inscription in Black Lettering occurs on both long sides and on either side of the cross-shaft. The inscription is quite worn and illegible.
Bibliography: Fitzgerald, W., 1903, 445.

24. GROUP: 6
A portion of a slab which measures 1.78m in length, .30m in width at its top, .27m in width at its base and .09m in average thickness. The sinister edge is chamfered and measures .04m in width. It lies in the chancel. Its decorated surface is weathered and chipped. The design is incised and what survives of the cross head consists of the lower segment of an outline circle, beneath which is a circular knop surmounting an outline cross-stem, which terminates in a stepped base. There is no evidence to suggest that the slab bore an inscription.
Bibliography: Unpublished..

25. GROUP: 4 Fig. 54
This tapered slab measures 1.84m in length, .60m in width at its top, .45m in width at its base and .07m in average thickness. The side and ends bear a chamfer which measures .02m in width. It lies in the chancel near the north wall. It survives in good condition, except for a small break in the lower dexter corner. The design consists of a seven-armed segmental cross carved in relief with simple fleur-de-lis terminals. Three cross-bands occur at the base of the cross-head, surmounting the cross-shaft. One single such band occurs at the base of the shaft, surmounting a pillar-base form. An inscription in Black Lettering occurs along both sides, across the top and base of the slab, and along the cross-shaft and base. It reads:

HIC IACET IVILLS? IKEARNY CONUBIUS CANCTI PATRICII A CASSELO QUI OBIIT VII DIE / MENSIS MAII / ANO DNI M CCCCC III CUI AIE PPICIET .... S ET PATRICIUS OKEARNY FILIIUS EIUS D....ET .... FIERI FECIT .....

(Here lies [Julius?] O'Kearny attendant [of the Church] of Saint Patrick of Cashel who died 7th day of May, A.D. 1503 on whose soul may God have mercy and Patrick O'Kearny, his son [who caused this tomb to be made?]).

Conubius is, perhaps, not classical Latin but Church Latin meaning 'Servant of God'?

Bibliography: Unpublished..

Site Name	St. Ruadhán's Abbey
Townland	Lorrha
SMR Site No.	T1004-010
N.G.R.	19196/20456

St. Brendan founded a monastery here but he moved to Clonfert following St. Ruadhán's arrival. The monastery became the subsequent site of a priory of Augustinian Canons, which appears to have been built north of the earlier church. It was burnt in 1157 and again in 1179. Maurice O'Kennedy was elected prior *c.*1436 but the pope issued a mandate in favour of Patrick O'Hanly who became prior. In 1450 Patrick was accused of misrule by Maurice Omurayn, one of the canons. Roderick Olachthain was prior in 1477. In 1552 a lease was granted to John O'Hogan, formerly prior of Larrowe in Ormond, for the priory of Canons of St. Augustine and the Dominican friary for twenty years. He may have allowed religious life to continue until after 1578 (Gwynn and Hadcock 1970, 185).

The fifteenth century Augustinian priory is entered by a very ornate west doorway. This doorway is surmounted by an ogee-headed moulding, it has moulded orders and is pointed. Above it is a two-light window of simple cusped tracery (Leask 1960, 76). There is a vaulted sacristy attached to the church. The medieval slabs lie in the chancel.

1. GROUP: 6
This tapered slab survives in two portions. The upper portion measures .55m in length, .62m in width and .11m in average thickness. The lower portion measures .69m in length, .53m in width and .10m in average thickness. It lies in the chancel near the south wall. The upper surface of the slab is worn and the design is difficult to decipher. It is composed of a broad outline cross-stem which is surmounted by the remains of what appears to have been an equal-armed cross with expanded terminals. Only the lower member of the latter element survives, the original upper portion of the slab being missing. On either side of the cross-stem two long rectangular areas are delineated by

grooves and broad recessed areas at the top and base. There is no evidence to suggest that the slab bore an inscription.
Bibliography: Unpublished.

Site Name	Two-Mile-Borris Church
Townland	Borris
SMR Site No.	T1042-05202
N.G.R.	21940/15780

Unfortunately no historical information was found for this site. All that remains is the village cemetery. No trace of the medieval church survives. Borris 1 stands at the east end of the old cemetery.

1. Group 2 Figs. 14b, 55
A tapered slab with a pointed top, measuring .87m in length, .49m in width near its top, .44m in width at its base and .17m in average thickness. It stands at the east end of the cemetery. A human head is carved in high relief at the top of the slab and it has a chevelure curling above the ears. Below the head is a floriated cross, carved in relief with a lozenge-shaped centre. There is no evidence on the slab to suggest that it bore an inscription, however, Hunt (1974, 232) states that there "seems to have been a very worn inscription on the sinister side. It is possibly in Black lettering and may have been added later". No traces of such survive.
Bibliography: Hunt, J., 1974, 231-2.

BIBLIOGRAPHY

Andersen, J., 1977. *The Witch on the Wall.* Copenhagen.

Anon, 1833. The Goban Saor, *The Dublin Penny Journal*, No. 66, Vol. 11, Oct. 5, 112.

Anon, 1898. County Kilkenny: Kells Parish, *Jour. of the Assoc. for the Preservation of the Memorials of the Dead*, IV, 81-82.

Anon, 1901. County Kilkenny: Kilree, *Jour. of the Assoc. for the Preservation of the Memorials of the Dead*, V, 86.

An Foras Forbartha, 1975. *Buildings of Architectural Interest in Co. Tipperary (S.R.).* Dublin.

Ariès, P., 1985. *Image of Man and Death* (translated by Janet Lloyd), Harvard.

Atkinson, E.D., 1906. County Galway: Clonfert Cathedral, *Jour. of the Assoc. for the Preservation of the Memorials of the Dead*, VI, 559.

Bagwell, R., and Clarke, W., 1890. County Tipperary: Parish of Clonmel, *Jour. of the Assoc. for the Preservation of the Memorials of the Dead*, IV, 239.

Bagwell, R., 1909. Innishlonagh Abbey, *Jour. Roy. Soc. Antiq. Ire.*, 39, 267-8.

Barry, T.B., 1977. *The Medieval Moated Sites of South-Eastern Ireland: Counties Carlow, Kilkenny, Tipperary and Wexford*, B.A.R. 35, Oxford.

Barry, T.B., 1987. *The Archaeology of Medieval Ireland.* London.

Bradley, J., 1985. The medieval tombs of St. Canice's. In: Empey, C.A. (ed.), *A Worthy Foundation: The Cathedral Church of St. Canice, Kilkenny, 1285-1985*, 54-103. Dublin.

Bradley, J., 1985. The medieval towns of Tipperary. In: Nolan, W. and McGrath, T.G. (eds.), *Tipperary: History and Society*, 34-59. Dublin.

Bradley, J., 1988. Anglo-Norman sarcophagi from Ireland. In: MacNiocaill, G. and Wallace, P.F.(eds.), *Keimelia*, 74-94. Galway.

Brennan, J., 1854-1855. Proceedings and Transactions, *Jour. of the Kilkenny Arch. Soc.*, 3, 214-215.

Burke, W., 1907.. *History of Clonmel*, Waterford, Reprinted in 1983 by Brethius Press, Kilkenny.

Butler, L.A.S., 1958. Some early northern grave covers - a reassessment, *Archaeologia Aeliana*, 36, 207-20.

Butler, L.A.S., 1964. Minor medieval monumental sculpture in the East Midlands, *Archaeological Jour.*, 121, 111-53.

Butler, L.A.S., 1987. Symbols on medieval memorials, *Archaeological Jour.*, 144, 246-55.

Cadogan Rothery, G., 1994. Concise Encyclopaedia of Heraldry. London.

Cairns, C.T., 1987. *Irish Tower Houses, a Co. Tipperary case study*, Dublin.

Carrigan, W., 1903. Kilcooley Abbey, *Jour. of the Assoc. for the Preservation of the Memorials of the Dead*, V, 452-7.

Champneys, A.C., 1910. *Irish Ecclesiastical Architecture*. Dublin, reprinted in 1970 by Irish Academic Press, Shannon..

Cook, R., 1974. *The Tree of Life: Image for the Cosmos*. London.

Crawford, H.S., 1909. Donaghmore Church, County Tipperary, *Jour. Roy. Soc. Antiq. Ire.*, 39, 261-70.

Crossley, F.H., 1921. *English Church Monuments A.D. 1150-1550*. London.

Curtis, E., 1935. Rental of the Manor of Lisronagh, 1333, *Proc. Roy. Ir. Acad.*, 43, 41-76.

Cutts, E.L., 1849. *A Manual for the Study of the Sepulchral Slabs and Crosses of the Middle Ages*. London.

Darling, Mr. 1895. County Cork: Kinsale Parish, *Jour. of the Assoc. for the Preservation of the Memorials of the Dead*, III, 43-7.

de Paor, L., 1956. The limestone crosses of Clare and Aran, *Jour. of the Galway Arch. and Hist. Soc.*, 26, 53-71.

Diringer, D., 1962. *Writing*. London.

Diringer, D., 1968. *The Alphabet: A Key to the History of Mankind*, 1, 418-35. London.

Doody, M.G., 1987. Ballyveelish 1, Co. Tipperary. Moated site. In: Cleary, R.M., Hurley, M.F., and Twohig, E.A. (eds.), *Archaeological Excavations on the Cork-Dublin Gas Pipeline*, 74-87. Cork.

Duport, M., 1934. La Sculpture Irlandaise a La Fin du Moyen Age, *La Revue de L'Art* 66, no. 355, 49-62.

Empey, C.A., 1970. The cantreds of medieval Tipperary, *North Munster Antiq. Jour.* 13, 23-29.

Empey, C.A., 1981. The Settlement of the Kingdom of Limerick, in J.F. Lydon (ed.) *England and Ireland in the Later Middle Ages*, 1-25. Dublin.

Empey, C.A., 1985. The Norman Period, 1185-1500, in W. Nolan and T.G.McGrath (eds.) *Tipperary: History and Society*, 71-91. Dublin.

Fitzgerald, W., 1901. Parish of Holy Cross: Holy Cross Abbey, *Jour. of the Assoc. for the Preservation of the Memorials of the Dead*, V, 102-8.

Fitzgerald, W., 1902. County Tipperary: Loughmore, *Jour. of the Assoc. for the Preservation of the Memorials of the Dead*, V, 258-63.

Fitzgerald, W., 1902. County Tipperary: Cashel Parish, St. John's Cathedral, *Jour. of the Assoc. for the Preservation of the Memorials of the Dead*, V, 247-51.

Fitzgerald,W., 1903. County Tipperary: Parish of Cashel, The Rock of Cashel, *Jour. of the Assoc. for the Preservation of the Memorials of the Dead*, V, 434-48.

Fitzgerald, W., 1908. Rathmore (St. Lawrence's Church and Burial-Ground), *Jour. of the Assoc. for the Preservation of the Memorials of the Dead*, VII, 424-44.

Fitzgerald, W., 1911. County Meath: Killeen Church ruins, *Jour. of the Assoc. for the Preservation of the Memorials of the Dead*, VIII, 401-18.

Fitzgerald,W., 1913/14. County Carlow: Tullow Churchyard, *Jour. of the Assoc. for the Preservation of the Memorials of the Dead*, IX, 19-20.

Ffrench, J.F.M., 1896. County Wexford: *Jour. of the Assoc. for the Preservation of the Memorials of the Dead*, 352-53.

Garstin, J.R., 1899. Wexford: Parish of New Ross, *Jour. of the Assoc. for the Preservation of the Memorials of the Dead*, IV, 320-37.

Garstin, J.R., 1899. County Wexford: North Transept, St. Mary's Church, *Jour. of the Assoc. for the Preservation of the Memorials of the Dead*, IV, 321-2.

Garstin, J.R., 1903. County Tipperary: Fethard, *Jour. of the Assoc. for the Preservation of the Memorials of the Dead*, V, 451.

Garstin, J.R., 1907. Waterford, the French Church, *Jour. of the Assoc. for the Preservation of the Memorials of the Dead*, VII, 190-1.

Gillespie, R., 1985. Funerals and society in early seventeenth century Ireland, *Jour. Roy. Soc. Antiq. Ire.*, 115, 86-91.

Gillespie, R., 1992. The Image of death, 1500-1700, *Arch. Ireland*, 6(1), 8-10.

Glasscock, R.E., 1970. Moated site and deserted borough and villages: Two neglected aspects of Anglo-Norman settlement in Ireland, in Stephens, N. and Glasscock, R.E., (eds.), *Irish Geographical studies in honour of E. Estyn Evans*, 162-177, Belfast.

Gough, J., 1786. *Sepulchral Monuments of Great Britain*, Vol. 1.

Gwynn, A., and Hadcock, R.N., 1970. *Medieval Religious Houses: Ireland.* Dublin.

Gwynn, A., 1992. *The Irish Church in the Eleventh Centuries.* Dublin.

Harbison, P., 1970. *Guide to the National Monuments of Ireland.* Dublin.

Harbison, P., 1989. *The Shell Guide to Ireland.* Dublin.

Hayes, W.J., 1970. *Burials in Holycross Abbey.* Holycross. Henry, F., 1970. *Irish Art in the Romanesque Period (1020-1170 A.D.).* London.

Hennessey, N., 1985. Parchial Organisation in Medieval Tipperary, in Nolan W. and McGrath T.G. (eds.) *Tipperary: History and Society*, 60-70. Dublin.

Henry, F., 1970. *Irish Art in the Romanesque Period. (1020-1170A.D.).* London.

Hewetson, J., 1902. Clonmel Parish: the "O'Donill" inscription, *Jour. of the Assoc. for the Preservation of the Memorials of the Dead*, V, 255-8.

Higgins, J.G., 1987. *The Early Christian cross slabs, pillar stones and related monuments of County Galway, Ireland.* (2 vols. Brit. Archaeol. Rep. S 375).

Hunt, J., 1974. *Irish Medieval Figure Sculpture 1200-1600.* Dublin/London.

Knowles, J.A., 1903. *Fethard Its Abbey and C.* Dublin.

Langrishe, R., 1905. Knocktopher Abbey, *Jour. of the Assoc. for the Preservation of the Memorials of the Dead*, VI, 364-6.

Leask, H.G., and Macalister, R.A.S., 1946. The partial excavation of a site at Liathmore or Leigh, County Tipperary, *Proc. Roy. Ir. Acad.*, 51C, 1-15.

Leask, H.G., 1951. *Irish Castles.* Dundalk.

Leask, H.G., 1955. *Irish Churches and Monastic Buildings I: Early Phases and the Romanesque.* Dundalk.

Leask, H.G., 1958. *Irish Churches and Monastic Buildings II: Gothic Architecture to A.D. 1400.* Dundalk.

Leask, H.G., 1960. *Irish Churches and Monastic Buildings III: Medieval Gothic, the Last Phases.* Dundalk.

Long, R.H., 1907. County Tipperary: Fethard, Church of the Holy Trinity, *Jour. of the Assoc. for the Preservation of the Memorials of the Dead*, VII, 175-83.

Macalister, R.A.S., 1909. *The Memorial Slabs of Clonmacnoise.* Dublin.

Macalister, R.A.S., 1913. The Dominican Church at Athenry, *Jour. Roy. Soc. Antiq. Ire.*, 33, 197-222.

Maher, D., 1990. A medieval grave-slab at Lisronagh, Co. Tipperary , *North Munster Antiq. Jour.* 34, 30-37.

Maher, D., 1992. A Medieval Grave-Slab at Lisronagh, Co. Tipperary, *North Munster Antiq. Jour.*, 34, 30-37.

Maher, D., 1994. Medieval Grave-Slabs at Derrynaflan, Co. Tipperary, *Tipperary Historical Journ.* 162-166.

Manning, T. White, 1902. County Kilkenny: Kilmacow Parish, *Jour. of the Assoc. for the Preservation of the Memorials of the Dead*, V, 227-9.

O'Connor, J., 1991. *Sheela Na Gig.* Fethard.

O'Donovan, J., 1840. *Ordnance Survey Letters.*

O'Farrell, F., 1980. Tomb slab (1626) at Lorrha, Co. Tipperary, *North Munster Antiq. Jour.*, 22, 63.

O'Farrell, F., 1983. Passion Symbols in Irish church carvings, *Old Kilkenny Review*, 2, 535-41.

O'Farrell, F., 1985. Incised slab at Athassel Priory, Co. Tipperary, *North Munster Antiq. Jour.*, 81-3.

O'Flanagan, M., 1930. Typescript of *Letters Containing Information Relating to the Antiquities of the Co. Tipperary: Collected During Progress of the Ordnance Survey in 1840.*

Ó Floinn, R., (forthcoming) Cross-slabs from Liathmore, in Manning, C. (ed.) *Dublin and Beyond the Pale: studies in honour of Patrick Healy.*

O'hOgain, D., 1985. *The Hero in Irish Folk History* (Dublin/New York) 264-5.

O'Keeffe, T., 1995. *Fethard, Co. Tipperary: An Archaeological & Historical Survey.* National Heritage Council.

O'Leary, E., 1928. Everard tomb, Fethard, Co. Tipperary, *Jour. Roy. Soc. Antiq. Ire.*, 18, 161-2.

Oliver, S., 1994. *An Introduction to Heraldry.* London.

Prim, J.G.A., 1851. On the discovery of ancient sepulchral monuments at the Dominican Abbey, Kilkenny, *Jour. Kilkenny Arch. Soc.*, I, 453-62.

Roe, H.M., 1966. Some aspects of medieval culture in Ireland, *Jour. Roy. Soc. Antiq. Ire.*, 97, 105-9.

Roe, H.M., 1968. Cadaver effigial monuments in Ireland, *Jour. Roy. Soc. Antiq. Ire.*, 98, 1-19.

Roe, H.M., 1983. Instruments of the Passion, *Old Kilkenny Review*, 2, 527-33.

Ryan, M., 1983. *The Derrynaflan Hoard 1: A Preliminary Account.* Dublin.

Ryder, P.F., 1985. *The Medieval Cross Slab Grave Cover in County Durham.* Durham.

Rynne, 1971., A Late Medieval Casket from Knockmore, Co. Clare, *North Munster Antiq. Jour.* XIV, 37-40.

Seymour, J. D., 1908. County Tipperary: Churches and church sites in the Barony of Eliogarty, County Tipperary, *Jour. of the Assoc. for the Preservation of the Memorials of the Dead*, VII, 458-66.

Shelley, P.B., 1798-1822. Ozymandias. In: Kennedy, P.J. (ed), *Senior Poetry: An Anthology of Matriculation and Leaving Certificate Poetry*, 131.

Stalley, R.A., 1971. *Architecture and Sculpture in Ireland, 1150-1350.* Dublin.

Stalley, R.A., 1987. *The Cistercian Monasteries of Ireland.* London.

Stephens, P., 1896. County Tipperary: Fethard, *Jour. of the Assoc. for the Preservation of the Memorials of the Dead*, III, 335-6.

Stout, G., 1984. Archaeological Survey of the Barony of Ikerrin, Roscrea.

Styan, K.E., 1902. *History of Sepulchral Cross-Slabs.* London.

Vigors, P.D., 1895. Keteller stone, Kilkenny, *Jour. Roy. Soc. Antiq. Ire.*, 5, 79-81.

Vigors, P.D., 1896. County Wexford. New Ross - St. Mary's Church, *Jour. of the Assoc. for the Preservation of the Memorials of the Dead*, III, 353.

Vigors, P.D., 1899. County Wexford. St. Mary's Church, *Jour. of the Assoc. for the Preservation of the Memorials of the Dead*, IV, 321-40.

Vigors, P.D., 1900. County Wexford: New Ross Parish - St. Mary's Church, *Jour. of the Assoc. for the Preservation of the Memorials of the Dead*, IV, 497-501.

Vigors, P.D., 1903. County Wexford: New Ross - St. Mary's Church, *Jour. of the Assoc. for the Preservation of the Memorials of the Dead*, V, 490-2.

Wallace, P.F., and Timoney, M.A., 1987. Carrowntemple, Co. Sligo and its inscribed slabs. In: Rynne, E (ed.) *Figures from the Past*, 43-62. Dublin.

Whelan, K., 1985. The Catholic Church in Co. Tipperary 1700-1900, in Nolan W. and McGrath, T.G., (eds.) *Tipperary: History and Society.* Dublin.

Yeats, W.B., 1865-1939. Sailing to Byzantium. In: Jeffares, A.N. (ed.), 1974, *Yeats Selected Poetry*, 105.

ILLUSTRATIONS

Fig. 24 Slab no.1, Athassel Augustinian Abbey.

Fig. 25 (left) Slab no.9, Athassel Augustinian Abbey.
Fig. 26 (right) Slab no. 1, Donaghmore Church.

Fig. 27 Slab no. 2, Donaghmore Church.

Fig. 28 Slab no. 9, Fethard Augustinian Abbey.

Fig. 29 Slab no.11, Fethard Augustinian Abbey.

Fig. 30 Slab no.13, Fethard Augustinian Abbey.

Fig. 31 Slab no. 2, Fethard Holy Trinity Church.

Fig. 32 (left) Slab no. 1, Fethard Holy Trinity Church.
Fig. 33 (right) Slab no. 3, Fethard Holy Trinity Church.

Fig. 34 Slab no.9, Holy cross Cistercian Abbey, in tomb niche.

Fig. 35 (left) Slab no.3, Kilcooley Cistercian Abbey.
Fig. 36 (right) Slab no. 4, Kilcooley Cistercian Abbey.

Fig. 37 (left) Slab no. 6, Kilcooley Cistercian Abbey.
Fig. 38 (right) Slab no. 1, Kiltinan Church.

Fig. 39 (left) Slab no. 1, Liathmore Church.
Fig. 40 (right) Slab no. 2, Marlfield Church.

Fig. 41 Slab no. 1, Old St. Mary's Church, Clonmel.

Fig. 42 Slab no. 3. Old St Mary's Church, Clonmel.

Fig. 43 (left) Slab no.9, St. Dominick's Priory, Cashel, positioned beneath pillar.
Fig. 44 (right) Slab no.1 St. Patrick's Cathedral, Cashel.

Fig. 45 (left) Slab no.4, St. Patrick's Cathedral, Cashel.
Fig. 46 (right) Slab no. 5, St. Patrick's Cathedral, Cashel.

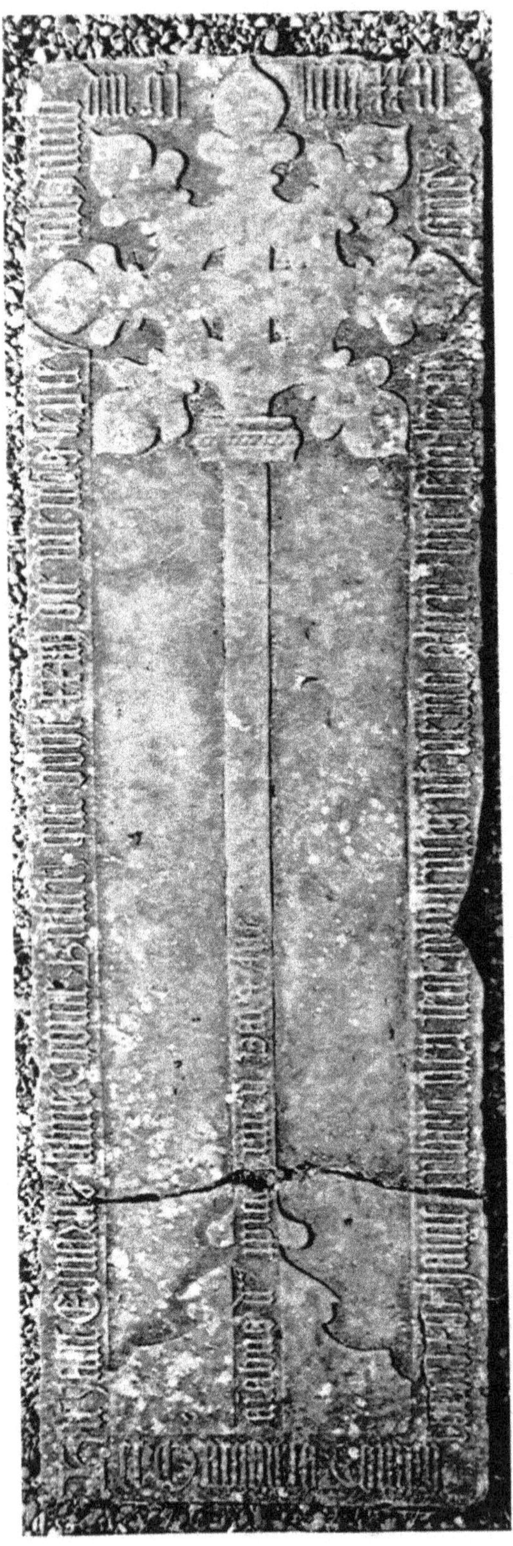

Fig. 47 (left) Slab no. 6, St. Patrick's Cathedral, Cashel
Fig. 48 (right) Slab no.9, St. Patrick's Cathedral, Cashel.

Fig. 49 (left) Slab no.15, St. Patrick's Cathedral, Cashel.
Fig. 50 (right) Slab no.16, St. Patrick's Cathedral, Cashel.

Fig. 51 Slab no.17, St. Patrick's Cathedral, Cashel.

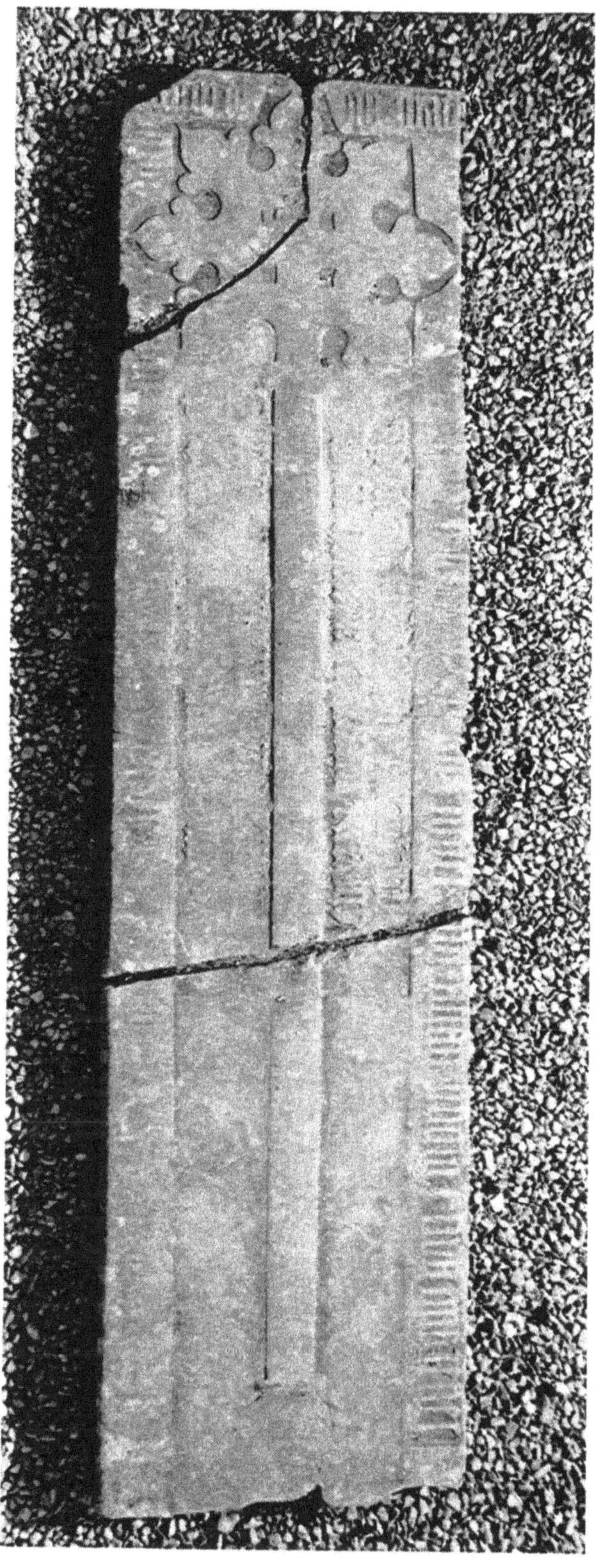

Fig. 52 Slab no.19, St. Patrick's Cathedral, Cashel.

Fig. 53 Slab no. 23, St. Patrick's Cathedral, Cashel.

Fig. 54 Slab no.25, St. Patrick's Cathedral, Cashel.

Fig. 55 Slab no.1, Two-Mile-Borris Church.

Fig. 56 Detail of Slab no.1, Old St. Mary's Church, Clonmel.

www.ingramcontent.com/pod-product-compliance
Lightning Source LLC
Chambersburg PA
CBHW061007030426
42334CB00033B/3400
* 9 7 8 0 8 6 0 5 4 9 2 3 9 *